To be a spiritual leade[barcode]g
a servant. This excell [MW00436057] ...ne
way. I wish I could place it in the hands of every pastor. They
would serve Christ and their church more faithfully.

Daniel L. Akin, president,
Southeastern Baptist Theological Seminary

The world measures success by metrics and outcomes. Sadly,
worldly success has influenced the church and even how
Christians approach serving the Lord. In *Servants for His Glory*,
Dr. Miguel Núñez argues that God calls us to a different standard. Our doing should flow out of our being. And if we are
to serve the Lord in a manner that seeks to make him, not us,
famous, we must do so in a manner that reflects his character.
If you long to be a useful servant that lives for God's glory, I
encourage you to pick up this book.

Juan R. Sanchez, senior pastor, High Pointe
Baptist Church, Austin, Texas and author of *The Leadership
Formula: Develop the Next Generation of Leaders in the Church*

So much of the literature on Christian leadership puts the pro-
verbial cart before the horse, focusing on the "how" of leadership
but skipping over some fundamental questions of identity. That's
why Servants for His Glory is so important. Miguel Núñez has
given Christian leaders a clear and urgent call, reminding us that
godly and effective leadership is most profoundly anchored in
what it means to know and follow the risen Christ.

Matthew J. Hall, provost and senior vice president of
Academic Administration, The Southern Baptist
Theological Seminary, Louisville, Kentucky

This book of wisdom, distilled from the pages of Scripture and
decades of faithful service in the church, offers help to those in
the pulpit and in the pew to learn how to be a servant. May this

book help all God's people learn how to serve from wellsprings of humility, courage, conviction, and grace. Ultimately, may it encourage us all to be sanctified servants, growing in holiness for the glory of God.

Stephen J. Nichols, president of Reformation Bible College and chief academic officer of Ligonier Ministries

In an age that has so much pontificating but so little learning, this text is full to bursting with wisdom. Written by a godly man who is an experienced pastor-theologian, it is surgically discerning and continually convicting. This is, quite simply, one of the best books on the Christian life I've ever read.

Owen Strachan, author of *Reenchanting Humanity* and *Always in God's Hands* and professor, Midwestern Seminary

SERVANTS
FOR HIS GLORY

DR. MIGUEL NÚÑEZ

SERVANTS FOR HIS GLORY

*Cultivating
Christlikeness
in a World of
Performance*

B&H
PUBLISHING
NASHVILLE, TENNESSEE

Wisdom&
Integrity
Collection

CONTENTS

INTRODUCTION

All literary works have both a motivation and an intention. Motivation is what moves the author to dedicate time and effort to write down the thoughts and ideas which have filled his mind so that they can be shared with others. Quite often, the author of a book spends years researching and reflecting on the subject about which he seeks to write, so much so that he is finally able to organize his ideas so they fit together like pieces of a jigsaw puzzle. At this point, many of us move forward in an effort to write for the benefit of others. Intention, on the other hand, deals more with what the author wishes to see accomplished in the life of his readers. It is possible that in some cases, his only intention is to entertain his readers, but in other cases, his goal is to contribute to the transformation of their lives. Such is the intention of the book you are reading.

As soon as you read the title of this book, you begin to have an idea of the subject matter discussed within it. I do not know how many people have noticed the interest that human beings have in doing something productive or significant. I believe that many of us are striving to do something which will convince us that our life counts, even as many place importance on knowing that they are leaving a legacy for their posterity. These feelings and emotions propel human beings into the world with the goal of accomplishing objectives, which requires them to participate in "doing things."

In general, we all come into this world with a certain void in our hearts, which produces a search for meaning. Each of us carries this out in different ways. Men, by nature, are doers and find their identity in what they accomplish. We see how little boys enjoy building sandcastles or forts or setting up toy soldiers on an imaginary battlefield. It would appear that men have been born both ready for battle and ready "to do" what is necessary.

On the opposite side of the spectrum, women are naturally inclined to develop and find their identity in personal relationships. Even as little girls, we see how some tend to play with their dolls at an early age and assume the role of mother without necessarily being taught how to live out or express motherhood. Nevertheless, as society has been steadily downplaying the value of motherhood, we have observed that many women have embraced life as professionals because they find more satisfaction in what they can do outside of the home as opposed to what they could do inside of the home in service to their families. "Doing" has become the addiction of the citizens of our generation.

It is both sad and concerning that while human beings are highly concerned with the things they accomplish, they do not place a high value on cultivating their inner being, which certainly would allow them to better manage the world around them. This explains the great failures we continuously see in everyday life, such as when an unprepared individual jumps at the opportunity to do something meaningful even though he is neither mature enough nor strong enough to stay the course in order to accomplish the goals and objectives of the task.

Human beings, in general, and men in particular, do not want to invest the time necessary for their formation. Rather, our first inclination is to want to be given responsibilities so that we can start accomplishing tasks immediately. It is as if we consider it a poor use of our time if we don't see work being accomplished. In other words, any time dedicated to the formation of the inner man is seen as a waste of time and effort. Accomplishing these tasks produces a sense of satisfaction in us and causes us to feel some form of significance. Something similar occurs when we finish our university career in our particular field of study; we develop a certain impatience because we experience the need to see ourselves active in our field of study. And certainly, part of our learning occurs when it is time to put into practice that which we have learned in theory.

In the Christian life, things are not that different at all. Someone is born again on the day of his conversion and frequently, almost immediately, he starts asking: "What can I do?" and when he hears that the best thing that he can do is to wait until he has grown in wisdom at the feet of Christ, he feels as if a bucket of cold water has been dumped on his head, and he might even be offended. This desire increases when we see others who are already doing something for God that we also desire to do. It is as if we have been programmed to "do" things, something that is particularly true for men. We must not forget that we are human "beings" and not human "doings." There is no doubt that having the motivation to serve is a good thing, but the question is if we are ready to carry out such service. When an individual's character has not been formed before he begins to serve, he can cause a lot of damage. The problem becomes even worse when the motivation to serve is neither good nor holy. No one begins serving with pure motivations. In fact, because no one is perfect and will not be perfect until we are called home to glory, we will often be serving with a certain level of corruption in our motivations. Occasionally, we are honest enough to admit it.

Much of what we will discuss in the coming chapters is based on my own personal growth and ongoing observation as a medical professional, pastor, and counselor. The topics that we will discuss most likely will not be foreign to us, as we have experienced some of them in our own lives while observing others in our relationships with friends, relatives, church members, patients, and acquaintances in general. We all walk down this same path.

CHAPTER I

You Must Be before You Do

The Twelve summoned the whole company of the disciples and said, "It would not be right for us to give up preaching the word of God to wait on tables. Brothers and sisters, select from among you seven men of good reputation, full of the Spirit and wisdom, whom we can appoint to this duty."

Acts 6:2–3

By nature, some of us are more observant than others. One activity that I enjoy is observing human behavior, which leads me to both reflect upon and view through the lens of God's revelation. I have always found it interesting how a child at a very early age struggles with his mother in an attempt to unsuccessfully tie his shoelaces all by himself without her help, repeating this cycle over and over again. He tries to complete this task even though he does not yet possess the fine motor skills to do so. Some of this has to do with rebelliousness, autonomy, and self-sufficiency, which are big stumbling blocks for us. Other times, however, it has to do with our wanting to do something that matters, as we said in the introduction to this book. Even children do not want to wait to grow up to do those things for which they are not yet qualified to do. Impatience has always characterized human beings. And while God never seems to be in a hurry, we have no desire to slow down. From here on, we will begin to emphasize the idea behind everything we will discuss on the pages to follow: we must *be* before we *do*, or we will suffer the consequences.

The context of the passage above is the sudden growth of the church and its leadership who found it necessary to delegate tasks, as they no longer could continue to do so given their multiple obligations. The task before them was relatively simple: waiting on tables and distributing food among their brethren, which may have ultimately included celebrating the Lord's Supper (something the early church would frequently do). And yet, for simple tasks such as these, the apostles established certain criteria related to the character of the people who would serve. In simple actions such as waiting on tables, we can see exactly how important it is for us "to be before we do." This is one of many examples we find all throughout the biblical revelation, as we will see later in the coming chapters.

We tend to serve in a ministry capacity as soon as we possibly can because it makes us feel useful. Unfortunately, serving before we are ready not only can lead us to error, but it can also lead to the deformation of our character when we take pride in ourselves. The author of Ecclesiastes reminds us that "There is an occasion for everything, and a time for every activity under heaven" (Eccles. 3:1) while also stressing that God "has made everything appropriate in its time" (v. 11).

During the apostle Paul's first missionary journey, he was accompanied by Barnabas and John Mark. When they arrived at Pamphylia, John Mark decided to separate from the group and return to Jerusalem (Acts 13:13). Later, Paul did not want to take Mark on his second missionary journey, precisely because Mark had deserted Paul in Pamphylia on the first journey. This caused a great conflict between Paul and Barnabas (Acts 15:36–40). The text does not specify the reasons that caused Paul to think this way, but it is quite possible that after this experience, the apostle felt very strongly that Mark was not ready for that kind of ministerial work. Perhaps he lacked the necessary strength of character that could be acquired over time. Eventually, this is the same Mark who would author the gospel that bears his name. Nevertheless, at an earlier stage in his life, the apostle Paul did not consider him ready for the ministry.

After his disagreement with Paul, Barnabas decided to take John Mark along with him, and they departed in the other direction. It is possible that Mark needed someone who would continue to invest in him until he could be completely mature and ready for the work to which God had called him. This fact demonstrates the wisdom of the author of Ecclesiastes in saying that there is a time for everything or event under the sun. It also serves as a good example to remind us that we are not always ready to serve in ministry even though we may think we are. This is the motivation of everything else you will read in this book.

Our Arrival into the Family of God

The Bible goes into great detail concerning how Adam's fall profoundly impacted the integrity of God's image in man. Our minds were darkened, our hearts were hardened, and our wills were enslaved. However, the Bible does not make a calculation of how every fallen family unit affects the development of each of the members within that family unit. Some members were abandoned by parents who did not assume their responsibilities as parents. Others were raped by relatives or acquaintances. Some were bullied, mocked, or rejected; others were physically abused. This has been true in the case of many wives and children. Knowing that the world is made up of millions of families, we could speak about millions of these kinds of situations throughout history and across continents.

This makes it clear that before we can serve the family of God, He must do a work of healing and growth within us. The

Bible calls this work *sanctification*. Our purpose is not, nor could it be, to present a therapeutic alternative to the problems we just mentioned. Rather, it is to raise awareness that, on the one hand, when it comes to serving, we need evidence that we have really matured enough to be able to carry out the job that we have been called to do. If someone is not ready to manage his own world, he will be much less ready to direct the world of others around him. Let us not fool ourselves. The apostle Peter and the other apostles thought they were ready to drink of the cup that the Lord Jesus would drink, and only a few short hours later, they abandoned Him. The Master's death and resurrection were two events that served to ultimately prepare them for the ministry ahead.

Let us look at some of the behaviors that demonstrate our spiritual and emotional immaturity:

> For my part, brothers and sisters, I was not able
> to speak to you as spiritual people but as people
> of the flesh, as babies in Christ. I gave you milk
> to drink, not solid food, since you were not
> yet ready for it. In fact, you are still not ready,
> because you are still worldly. For since there is
> envy and strife among you, are you not worldly
> and behaving like mere humans? (1 Cor. 3:1–3)

Let us imagine for a moment, as may have occurred, that certain people with these types of characteristics had been chosen to serve in the church at Corinth. This explains, at least in part, the chaos surrounding the use of the gifts of the Spirit, an issue that the apostle Paul addresses in chapters 12 and 14 of the same letter.

The best evidence of the need for growth in the Christian before beginning to do anything for God is found in both of Paul's letters to the Corinthian church, as we can see in the text above. Let us begin our analysis of the text: "For my part, brothers and sisters, I was not able to speak to you as spiritual people but as people of the flesh, as babies in Christ" (1 Cor.

3:1). Here, Paul is confronting these brothers and sisters because, even though they were believers, he could not speak to them as mature believers but as immature children or individuals who were still of the world. Note how Paul equates these two things: people of the flesh and children. When he speaks of children, he is referring more to immaturity than to innocence. Their emotional and spiritual immaturity made them react in the flesh, as if they were still unbelievers. Paul continues:

> I gave you milk to drink, not solid food, since you were not yet ready for it. In fact, you are still not ready, because you are still worldly. For since there is envy and strife among you, are you not worldly and behaving like mere humans? (1 Cor. 3:2–3)

While Paul was with them, the Corinthians behaved like children. Therefore, Paul gave them milk to drink; that is, he spoke to them about simple things that they could understand. A little later, the apostle wrote and sent the letter we know today as his second epistle to this church, and even in that letter, we find evidence of immaturity within the church at Corinth. This was a church that was so immature or so carnal in its ways that it caused Paul to weep (2 Cor. 2:4).

In the same epistle, Paul leads them to understand that none of us has sufficient reason or status to be proud, because we are mere servants of Christ:

> For whenever someone says, "I belong to Paul," and another, "I belong to Apollos," are you not acting like mere humans?
>
> What then is Apollos? What is Paul? They are servants through whom you believed, and each has the role the Lord has given. I planted, Apollos watered, but God gave the growth. So, then, neither the one who plants nor the one who

> waters is anything, but only God who gives the
> growth. (1 Cor. 3:4–7)

Ultimately, neither Apollos, nor Paul, nor we are anything. This is a mature way of looking at life, so that tomorrow, when our brother or sister who possesses a gift and a talent is recognized and commended at church, let us not be jealous of him or condemn him. Let us not be envious of him or judge him. This is all part of God's plan for His church. Let us applaud our brother or sister to whom God has given something special.

In order to emphasize the importance of the growth that should occur in us as believers, let us take another look at a 1 Corinthians 3:2–3, but from the version of the Bible known as the New Living Translation (NLT):

> I had to feed you with milk, not with solid food,
> because you weren't ready for anything stronger.
> And you still aren't ready, *for you are still con-
> trolled by your sinful nature.* You are jealous of one
> another and quarrel with each other. Doesn't that
> prove you are controlled by your sinful nature?
> *Aren't you living like people of the world?* (emphasis
> added)

This section is key. We still have a sinful nature (the flesh), but that sinful nature should not control us. Some individuals control it better than others, depending on the level of sanctification they have reached. When we are under the great influence and control of our sinful nature, we may often find that jealousy, envy, strife, division, condemnation, and criticism are present; and that is what this text is presenting. Imagine that, in the midst of fights like the ones mentioned, you start to lead a youth or couples' group, or some other ministry in your church. The magnitude of the damage could be great, as often has been the case in many congregations. "[The Corinthians] were so entrenched in worldly ways of thinking that it was going to take a long time before they could tolerate 'solid food.'"[1]

Each of us is born insecure, and such insecurity makes us proud. But as Andrew Murray said, "Pride must die in you, or nothing of heaven can live in you."[2] Pride is just one of the many manifestations of our lack of maturity or lack of sanctification.

How Do We Enter into the Family of God?

1. We enter the Christian life as born again but affected by our past.

The day we give our lives over to the Lord, we become new creations, yet we still have a past that has shaped us and continues to manifest itself in our outer world. We come into the Christian life having been emotionally affected by our upbringing, education, past experiences, painful experiences, sometimes situations of incest, physical mistreatment, verbal mistreatment, superiority or inferiority complexes, and many other types of experiences. The reality is that each of us has been affected. Even after years in the faith, there is no guarantee that these things have left us unless we have grown, something which does not happen naturally. The first thing we must do is to accept that we come to the feet of Christ as individuals affected by our past.

2. We need to accept that we have been affected by our past so that we can deal with our sinful dysfunctionality.

If we do not accept that we have been affected by our past experiences, we will have the tendency to blame others instead of understanding why we are the way we are or why we feel the way we feel, only then to seek after God and His Word so that we may find the way of redemption of the image of Christ in us. In reality, there are people who have influenced who we are now, but once we enter into the Christian life, God wants us to deal with who we are so that we can begin to change. "We do not see things as they are. We see things as we are."[3]

3. We enter the Christian life with a distorted and unbiblical worldview.

Even though it may sound redundant, our worldview when we become a Christian is "worldly." Perhaps we could say that our worldview before coming to Christ is secular, but I do not believe that such a term sufficiently describes it. According to the *Merriam-Webster* dictionary, *secular* may refer to worldly things, but it may also describe things that are not overly religious. On the other hand, *Merriam-Webster* indicates that *worldly* deals with a relation or devotion to the pursuits of the world instead of religious or spiritual affairs. Therefore, we certainly enter into the Christian life with a worldview that is, without a doubt, of this world. We place value on our professions, our studies, how we dress, those with whom we have relationships, and we judge everyone else just like the rest of the world does. This is what we have known throughout the years. The problem is that unless we know and accept this reality, we will not be able see the difference between the biblical worldview and the "worldly" worldview in order to change it. This is the heart of the problem. It is common for us to listen to Sunday's sermon with a biblical worldview, only to then live our lives the rest of the week with a "worldly" worldview.

Worldview is how we see the world, how we judge it, and how we react to it. This worldview must be changed. We enter into the Christian life with incorrect perceptions, and if there is anything from which we suffer, it is precisely the following: we live with incorrect perceptions even years after we begin our Christian life. The only One who has a completely correct perspective of all that is seen and all that occurs is God. The question that we must ask ourselves is: "How incorrect are our perceptions?" Those of us who are counselors could say that the norm for human beings is to have an incorrect perception of reality. We see an example of this when we listen to a husband speak about a situation he is experiencing in his marriage and later listen to his wife describe the situation with a completely different perspective. At that moment, we could certainly wonder if these two individuals are really married or not. The husband describes the situation as being white, and the wife describes it as being black–two entirely different descriptions. In these cases, we see that between spouses distinct perceptions exist which frequently are each incorrect to some degree or another.

We have a self-centered worldview. We are the center of our universe, and this self-centered way of seeing things makes us ungrateful. After being given so much from God, family members, and friends, we do not respond with sufficient gratitude. The same thing also occurs within the church. Pastors, leaders, and other Christians all provide spiritual counsel and aid, only for us to respond with ungrateful hearts. Ingratitude is not part of the character of Christ; therefore, this all must change. If this form of thinking and acting does not change, we will begin to sinfully and erroneously teach others. We teach by both word and action.

4. We enter the Christian life with an overvaluation of ourselves.

We think we are worth more than we actually are. This is why we tend to judge and condemn others because, as we do so, we are able to tacitly affirm that we are superior to them. Perhaps we may have never preached a sermon, but we assume that we could do a much better job than the one who is preaching. God knows this about us, which is why He gave us the following instruction:

> For by the grace given to me, I tell everyone among you not to think of himself more highly than he should think. Instead, think sensibly, as God has distributed a measure of faith to each one. (Rom. 12:3)

This is our sinful tendency. Paul again insisted the same to the church at Corinth when he wrote:

For we don't dare classify or compare ourselves with some who commend themselves.
But in measuring themselves by themselves and
comparing themselves to themselves, they lack
understanding. (2 Cor. 10:12)

How Do We Evaluate Ourselves?

As we seek to be sincere, with the help of God and the Spirit
of God, we are able to continue discovering the signs of immaturity in our character. Some of these signs are:

1. A profound need for approval

Due to our fallen condition, we all long for approval.
Nevertheless, some of us have an extreme need for approval.
At the slightest hint of someone's disapproval of us, we become
offended and irritated, even when someone does not greet us,
for example. Other times the need is a little more hidden. "Even
public sharing of repentance and failure may be motivated by an
unconscious hunger for approval."[4] We are complex persons with
multiple tactics and defense mechanisms that serve to conceal
our dysfunctions. At the heart of it all, these external manifestations correspond to internal insecurities. We need a greater perspective of the God we worship and a smaller idea of man and
the recognition or accolades of this life. One reason why we sin
is that we crave the approval of people, or we fear their rejection.
We need the acceptance of others, and so we're controlled by
them. The Bible's term for this is "the fear of man."[5]

2. Perfectionism

Perfectionism is a sign of insecurity. As we experience a
greater level of insecurity, we experience a greater need to feel
secure. Perfectionism is nothing more than an external form of
wanting control over our environment because controlling our

environment guarantees our security, which is something we will never really attain. As we mature in our relationship with God, perfectionism should diminish as we feel more and more secure in Christ. When we place our life on the scale to be weighed, we learn that we are not as good as we think we are, and we are worse than we could ever imagine.

3. Jealousy

Jealousy is another indication that our emotional world must mature. Some people experience jealousy for friendships when others are able to make friends. The jealous person desires to control the relationships of others. Frequently, children experience this feeling when their parents have a second child. Some regress in their behavior, and we even see children between the ages of eight to ten years old start wetting the bed at night again. Such is our fallen condition. Where there is jealousy, there will inevitably be strife (1 Cor. 3:3; 2 Cor. 12:20; Gal. 5:20; James 3:14, 16).

4. Frequent Condemnation of Others

This attitude is motivated by a sense of superiority over others. We could also call this self-righteousness or moral arrogance. These individuals tend to point out or criticize anyone who does not live up to their standards. Mature people are humble people, and humble people do not feel the need to condemn others around them.

5. Resentment and Lack of Forgiveness

Resentment and lack of forgiveness are evidence of built-up anger, which is a warning sign of profound areas of immaturity. Emotionally mature people forgive others relatively easily. Even non-Christians who are emotionally mature are able to arrive at the point where they can forgive relatively easily, because man has been created in the image of God. Maybe those non-believers who manage to forgive others cannot forgive as deeply as a child of God or with the added blessings of being a child of God. Those who have difficulty forgiving see themselves as victims, and they forget that the greatest victim of all was the Lord Jesus, and we were His offenders.

6. Uncontrollable Outbursts of Anger

Outbursts of anger which we cannot control reveal a lack of self-control. This lack of control is more related to our fleshly nature than with the image of the new man. If we cannot control our anger, there is something in our sinful nature seizing control instead of the Holy Spirit who dwells within the believer. Let us remember that self-control is a fruit of the Spirit (Gal. 5:22–23). Anger in a father or mother produces profound damage within the family. We can say the same when anger forms part of the character of the leadership in the church. "In any event, our anger arises from our value system. It expresses our beliefs and motives."[6]

7. Loving to Serve, but for the Wrong Reasons

When we love to serve, but for the wrong reasons, we reveal our self-centeredness. We often love to serve others because doing so makes us the center of attention and, in our immaturity, we like being at the center. When we are the center of attention, people see us, they applaud us, they approve of us, and so on. We should serve, but we should do so for the right reasons. "Many people change their behavior, but their motives and desires are still wrong; so their new behavior is no more pleasing to God than their old behavior."[7]

When we do not serve and are on the periphery, we feel rejected, minimized, and worthless. The reality is that there is a time to be on the periphery and a time to be serving.

8. Difficulty Recognizing the Talent of Others

When we have difficulty recognizing talent in others, which is nothing more than a sign of envy, we justify ourselves with phrases such as, "I cannot applaud others because they could become proud." But in the Bible the reality is that we frequently find God commending many of His children. It is said that Moses was a very humble man, more so than any other on the face of the earth (Num. 12:3). Of Job, God says that he was a just and upright man (Job 1:8). Paul exhorts the brethren to imitate Timothy (1 Cor. 4:16–17). If we have learned anything, it is that we must not try to keep others humble because this is not our role. Our role is to encourage, edify, motivate, and help others. God will take care of the rest. This enables us to appreciate the talents of others.

9. Difficulty Controlling the Tongue

Difficulty controlling one's tongue reveals a lack of being filled with the Spirit. This is a sinful weakness that James discusses in chapter 3 of the epistle which bears his name. Lack of dominion over the tongue is not only sinful, but it also indicates a spiritual immaturity that is at the root of such a lack of control of our speech. The fruit of the Spirit (Gal. 5:22–23) is the result of being filled with the same Spirit. James reminds us:

> So too, though the tongue is a small part of the body, it boasts great things. Consider how a small fire sets ablaze a large a forest. And the tongue is a fire. The tongue, a world of unrighteousness, is placed among our members. It stains the whole body, sets the course of life on fire, and is itself set on fire by hell. (James 3:5–6)

10. Difficulty Maintaining Close Relationships with Those Who Differ from Us

This is very significant. Others do not have to be in agreement with our values, our likes, and our preferences. Many people distance themselves from those who differ from them because they feel insecure when they are around them; while others only know one way to relate to others, which is through codependency. In order to feel comfortable, codependent individuals need to be in agreement in everything. Codependency is frequently a sign that we have an extreme need for approval from other people whom we need for our sense of identity. Control is a prominent characteristic of codependent relationships.[8]

11. A Suspicious Attitude toward Others

There are individuals all around us who are suspicious of others. They pass value judgments and evaluate the intentions of others as if they were living inside them. These are the ones who are always putting puzzles together or playing chess with other people in their mind. Such an attitude leads to manipulation. We must not live this way. We cannot live a peaceful and tranquil life constantly rearranging the jigsaw puzzle or the chessboard. If we are emotionally mature, we rest in knowing God is the one who moves the chess pieces. It may be that at a certain moment, people are playing games with us, but it is best to let God be in charge of those games. Let us enjoy the peace and tranquility that a close relationship with God provides.

We need to have an emotionally mature life in order to experience the abundant life that Christ purchased for us (John 10:10). Our desire is that people would lead lives free of all of the snares that these fears cause. There is nothing better than to live emotionally free, in Christ and by Christ and not in our own strength. Can you imagine the damage we can cause if we live shackled by some of the things we have just mentioned? Sadly, this is the reality of many divided churches today.

The Need for Time

The biblical account allows us to see different ways of "being before doing." Moses spent forty years in the desert and, prior to that, he spent forty in the palace of the king of Egypt. God began using him as His prophet eighty years after he had been born. What did Moses do during all of that time in the desert? What did he learn? He certainly learned a lot because serving forty years in the sand and under the direction of his father-in-law (Jethro) has the tendency to produce humility in a person, something that, in effect, occurred—as the Word of God reveals that Moses was the most humble man on the face of the earth, as we mentioned earlier. In Pharaoh's palace, Moses was treated as a prince, but in the desert, he was simply a shepherd of sheep. Thus, Moses learned humility; he learned to serve; and he learned to follow. If you have not learned to follow others, you are not ready to lead. Believe me. There has not been one leader who was not first a good follower.[9] Joshua was formed in Moses' shadow, Elisha under the leadership of Elijah, and Timothy was trained by Paul. The good follower learns submission, humility, and patience, while also learning to listen. The great leaders have always learned all of this prior to being used greatly by God.

The testimony of the Old Testament demonstrates that reaching maturity and becoming a servant takes time. Even so, the reality is that none of us will become a Moses; therefore, forty years in the desert is not necessary for us. Thank God! But we do, in fact, need time; and if we continue to examine the life of this great prophet of God, we will observe another way in which God demonstrates the fact that we need a time of preparation and a work in our character before beginning to serve. When Moses is overloaded with work, Jethro, an older and probably more emotionally mature man, appears and provides Moses the following counsel:

But you should select from all the people able
men, God-fearing, trustworthy, and hating dishonest profit. Place them over the people as
commanders of thousands, hundreds, fifties, and
tens. (Exod. 18:21)

Note of Jethro's words: "able men, God-fearing, trustworthy,
and hating dishonest profit [bribes]." These men had already
arrived at the point of "being before doing." Before serving, in
their character, these men had to exhibit the characteristics cited
in the text.

The New Testament is no different. In one of his epistles,
Paul instructs Timothy, his youngest disciple, regarding when
to place people into service and what type of people should
serve. We know that there are diverse types of service, and some
require more time than others or require more character than
others; but at the end of the day, the idea is the same: in order
to serve, there should be a time of formation and preparation of
character. If our character has not been formed, the best thing
we can do is wait for it to be prepared. In this sense, Paul tells
Timothy in his second letter: "What you have heard from me
in the presence of many witnesses, commit to faithful men who
will be able to teach others also" (2 Tim. 2:2). Here we see that
the ability of these men to teach others (doing) is preceded by
faithfulness and competence that is observed in them (being).
What Paul is seeking to communicate to Timothy is: "Timothy,
when you come to the point of selecting people who will teach,
pay careful attention to their character, and as you do so, think
about those who are faithful, competent, and ideally suited. Then
you will be able to permit them 'to do' something . . . to teach."
The order is: character first, then service. This is very important
for us to note.

God's appointed leaders do not develop their integrity after
being appointed. Their integrity precedes them. We can see this
in the counsel that Jethro gave to his son-in-law, Moses; in Paul's
words to Timothy; and we see it in the requirements of being

an elder. A pastor or an elder "must not be a new convert, or he might become conceited and incur the same condemnation as the devil" (1 Tim. 3:6). A person should wait a while after his conversion before aspiring to be an elder. The first condition of being an elder is that the candidate must be "above reproach" (1 Tim. 3:2). When someone begins to serve, he can be sure that there will be much responsibility, and with responsibility comes power, influence, privileges, and rights which the character of the immature will not be ready to handle.

Again, we can see that the testimony of the Scriptures is that character is required in order to handle service, rights, privileges, influence, and power. God's grace is what makes possible all that we get to do; but once we move from God's grace to something more earthly, we could say that everything is related to character, and the formation of character takes time. Our God is never in a hurry, as we have already said. The Bible is Christ-centered from beginning to end, and still, when Christ came, He had to wait some thirty years to preach His first sermon. The One who is the subject and object of the entire biblical revelation had to wait thirty years. Why? Because His time had not yet come. God has a time for everything under the sun, but man wants things to be done according to his own time line. Jesus lived His life in a different way:

> After this, Jesus traveled in Galilee, since he did not want to travel in Judea because the Jews were trying to kill him. The Jewish Festival of Shelters was near. So his brothers said to him, "Leave here and go to Judea so that your disciples can see your works that you are doing. For no one does anything in secret while he's seeking public recognition. If you do these things, show yourself to the world." (For not even his brothers believed in him.)
>
> Jesus told them, "My time has not yet arrived, but your time is always at hand." (John 7:1–6)

Paul waited some seven to ten years after his Damascus road experience to take his first missionary journey. In the Old Testament, God stipulated thirty years of age as the minimum age at which a priest could serve. We do not believe that God randomly chose that age, because our God is a God of purpose. Without a doubt, in the history of the church there have been people who began serving God as prophets and preachers even during their adolescence. Jeremiah was one of those prophets, and Charles Spurgeon was one of those preachers. But we have not had many Jeremiahs, nor have we had many Spurgeons. Moreover, the exception does not create the rule.

God has emphasized character development all throughout His revelation. When Paul writes to Timothy, he says, "Don't let anyone despise your youth" (1 Tim. 4:12a). And he then immediately adds: "but set an example for the believers in speech, in conduct, in love, in faith, in purity" (v. 12b). Paul seems to say: Timothy, I urge you, even in your youth, to be an example . . .

>   *in speech* . . . when you speak
>
>   *in conduct* . . . in your lifestyle
>
>   *in love* . . . in what or how you feel
>
>   *in faith* . . . in what you believe
>
>   *in purity* . . . in what you see and do

In all of this, Timothy was to be an example, and today, we must do the same. Even in our youth, God places an emphasis on character above all for those who desire to serve Him. Character is what will sustain us in crisis. We must represent God well before men. Even this simple example allows us to see how important it is for us "to be before we do."

As we saw at the beginning of this chapter, when the early church began to grow, it was necessary to delegate some of the tasks that the apostles had been doing up to that point. Then we see that after the church had grown to several thousand people in number, it was necessary to include others who could help carry out the ministry. On one hand, this delegation of functions was motivated by various complaints that had come from some of the Hellenistic widows. Let us look at the following passage:

> Now in these days when the disciples were increasing in number, a complaint by the Hellenists arose against the Hebrews because their widows were being neglected in the daily distribution. And the twelve summoned the full number of the disciples and said, "It is not right that we should give up preaching the word of God to serve tables. Therefore, brothers, pick out from among you seven men of good repute, full of the Spirit and of wisdom, whom we will appoint to this duty. But we will devote ourselves to prayer and to the ministry of the word." (Acts 6:1–4 ESV)

For a task as simple as serving tables, it was necessary to choose individuals who had both a right walk with God, as well as a good testimony before men. Note how the text describes the people who should take on this task: "of good repute, full of the Spirit and of wisdom." This also means that God was emphasizing the need to cultivate our character before we serve in the kingdom of heaven.

Final Reflection

The Bible uses just one word to describe the way in which we grow. That word is *sanctification*, which describes the progressive process through which God makes us empty ourselves of the ways of thinking and the life habits that characterized the old man so that He may incorporate the image of the new man in us. This is produced by the sanctifying power of the Holy Spirit, as Paul so well describes in his Second Letter to the Corinthians:

> We all, with unveiled faces, are looking as in a
> mirror at the glory of the Lord and are being
> transformed into the same image from glory to
> glory; this is from the Lord who is the Spirit.
> (2 Cor. 3:18)

As we examine the Scriptures, the Spirit of God reveals areas
of sin in our lives and, by means of the same action of the Spirit,
He helps us to rid ourselves of everything that does not look like
Christ. This is a cooperative action of both the Word and the
Spirit of God. This is why Christ prayed in the following manner:

> Sanctify them by the truth; your word is truth.
> (John 17:17)

Now, in practical terms, what we continue to observe during
the process of sanctification could appear similar to what has
been described as the four stages of learning any new skill:[10]

1. Unconsciously unskilled

We do not know how to act or live well, and we are not aware
of it. In other words, "we do not know what we do not know."
Someone has to show us that we are bad. The Word of God and
the Spirit of God are primary agents of revealing areas of sin in
our lives, but God also uses people within His church to show us
our sin and guide us to the Truth.

2. Consciously unskilled

In this stage, we are aware of our sin, but we still have not
been able to overcome it because not enough time has passed
since being illuminated by the Word and the Holy Spirit to
implement in our lives the spiritual disciplines which are necessary to weaken the residual sin of the old man.

3. Consciously skilled

After a while, the Holy Spirit develops the character of Christ in us. He does so in such a way that the specific area of sin we have been dealing with continues to be left behind, but we will still have to consciously struggle against it. For example, if we are going to confront someone about his sin, we may need a lot of prayer and a reminder that we must be gracious if our natural tendency has been to be vengeful; but we are capable of achieving this, which is why we talk about being consciously skilled.

4. Unconsciously skilled

Finally, when God has cultivated the fruit of the Spirit in us, we may then become men and women who are controlled by the Holy Spirit, who now possess a transformed heart and mind, who behave as true sons and daughters of God because we have actually become something, by God's grace. We are not just doing things the right way ("doing without being"). Now, we think through His Word and act according to the Spirit. Now the fruit of the Spirit has been harvested:

> . . . [L]ove, joy, peace, patience, kindness, good-
> ness, faithfulness, gentleness, and self-control.
> The law is not against such things. (Gal. 5:22b–23)

Carrying out what we are proposing means change, and therefore, growth. For the Christian, being born again without growing is not an option, which is why we need a community of believers. We cannot grow in isolation.[11]

CHAPTER 2

Be a Servant Whose Inner World Is in Order

*Pay careful attention, then, to how you walk—not
as unwise people but as wise—making the most
of the time, because the days are evil. So don't be
foolish, but understand what the Lord's will is.*

Ephesians 5:15–17

Introduction

The outer world in which we live is a reflection of our inner
world, something which few recognize. Until our inner world is
in order, it will be impossible for us to get our lives in order. We
usually do things in reverse: we want to get our outer world *in*
order while our inner world is still *out* of order.

As the story goes, on one occasion a little girl approached
her father when he arrived home from work and asked him if
he would please play with her. The father was tired and wanted
to watch TV for a few hours. When his favorite program came
on, the little girl became insistent, and the father thought that

he could keep her entertained by giving her a few pencils and a coloring book. The little girl entertained herself for a little while but then returned to her father with the same request. The father looked around and discovered a newspaper with a map of the world printed on one of its pages. He then had an idea. He cut the map into several pieces, placed the pieces on a tray, gave the little girl a roll of tape, and asked the girl to "put the map of the world together again." Shortly thereafter, the little girl came back with the reassembled map. She did this so quickly that it surprised the father. He then asked her, "Sweetheart, how did you do it?" The daughter responded, "Behind the map of the world, there is a picture of a man. When you put the man together, you put the world together." This story might not have ever happened, but it perfectly illustrates how the human being desires to put his outer world in order without ever having put his inner world in order.

There are many reasons why a person's inner world becomes out of order, but in my opinion, the common denominator among all other denominators is poor use of time, which is also due to poor organization of priorities. This is why the apostle Paul instructs the Ephesians to make the most of their time. The reason he gives them for doing so, according to the biblical text quoted above, is because "the days are evil." If this was true in the first century, we can certainly say that the days are even worse in our generation, which seems not to believe in absolute values and questions all authority. When we do not make the most of our time, we are unwise and foolish, as the apostle Paul points out in the text above.

How we use our time is vital. We will never again be able to use yesterday's unused time. We cannot recover the time that we didn't use yesterday, nor will we ever be able to use it again. In other words, we are not living on the other side of glory where we will have an eternity before us. Our time is limited; we live on the side of eternity where our days are numbered. To make things even worse, we live in a world of great sin, much contamination, and an abundance of moral corruption. Therefore, if we do not make the best use of our time, we will end up suffering grave consequences.

The use of our time depends upon our worldview. As you recall, we briefly spoke about this topic in the previous chapter. The word *worldview* is a compound word consisting of *world* and *view*. Our worldview is certainly how we see the world. However, it is not only how we see the world but how we see life, as well. The word *worldview* was first coined by Immanuel Kant, and the original word in German is *Weltanschauung*, which implies a view or vision of the world and life.[1]

We have an incorrect view of this world and life; therefore, this distorted vision causes us to live in error and is what leads us to frequently desire to serve before we are ready. A person's worldview is key because it will determine how he thinks, what he desires, how he makes decisions, and it will even determine the goals he pursues and the purposes of his entire life. And finally, all of the elements we have mentioned establish how we use our time.

Our worldview either creates problems for us or avoids adverse consequences for us. We continually think, see, react, and relate to others through a worldview. This is why a proper worldview is something that we must have. Our worldview is the lens through which we see everything: the world and life. Imagine a photography camera with an out-of-focus lens. Everything looks distorted. Then, we adjust the focus of the lens until we've gained the correct focus, and everything looks as it should. This is how we frequently view life: distorted. The only thing that straightens out life and brings it into focus is the Word of God applied in our lives by means of the Holy Spirit. This requires us to consume the Scriptures and to be in communion with God. Both things are needed. Thus, in order to "be" before we "do," we must consume the Word of God and have an intimate communion with the Holy Spirit of God because, when these two things come together, our lens will be able to focus

well. It isn't until our life lens is in complete focus that we can do
what we have been called to do.

Our decisions reveal who we are and determine what we will
become. A decision that we make tomorrow may determine who
we will be within a year, be it good or bad; and that decision that
we make tomorrow will depend entirely upon a worldview.

The Christian Worldview Puts Our Inner World in Order

In the text of Ephesians 5:15–17, the apostle Paul exhorts us
to make the best use of the time. The word translated as time is
kairos, which, in this case, means that "he is talking about a great
moment."[2] It is a window of opportunity. In Greek, there are two
distinct words for time" one is *cronos* and the other is *kairos*. The
first has to do with chronology, the time which is measured on a
clock or the time related to the calendar, but this is not the word
used here in this text. The word that appears in the biblical text
we are considering is *kairos*, which, as we stated earlier, refers to
a special period or window of opportunity during which we may
accomplish certain things; but that window will eventually close.

Perhaps we have not considered the fact that there will come
a time when we will not be able to preach or minister. But that
time will certainly come. There will come a time when our children will leave home, and we will not be able to influence them
like we did before. There is a window of opportunity that will
close. In a general way, Paul says, "Make the best of your time,
and do not be foolish."

We said before that our worldview determines how we live.
John Piper best expresses what we are considering when he says:

> We must cultivate the mind-set of exiles. What
> this does mainly is sober us up and wake us up
> so that we don't drift with the world and take for
> granted that the way the world thinks and acts is
> the best way. We don't assume that what is on TV

is helpful to the soul; we don't assume that the priorities of advertisers are helpful to the soul; we don't assume that the strategies and values of business and industry are helpful to the soul. We don't assume that any of this glorifies God. We stop and we think and we consult the Wisdom of our own country, heaven, and we don't assume that the conventional wisdom of this age is God's wisdom. We get our bearings from God in his Word.

When you see yourself as an alien and an exile with your citizenship in heaven and God as your only Sovereign, you stop drifting with the current of the day. You ponder what is good for the soul and what honors God in everything: food, cars, videos, bathing suits, birth control, driving speeds, bed times, financial savings, education for the children, unreached peoples, famine, refugee camps, sports, death, and everything else. Aliens get their cue from God and not the world.[3]

The Call Is to Meditate on What Is Good for the Soul

Have you ever sat down to meditate on what is good for your soul and primarily on what honors God? For example, forms of entertainment that do not please God; movies that we enjoy but offend the image of God: vulgar speech; immodest or ostentatious ways of dressing; lifestyles that more resemble those who do not know the Lord than of those who have been created in the image of God. None of this is beneficial to our soul nor does it honor God. Pastor Piper gives us examples from everyday life which ought to cause us to think. Whatever we do or do not do with these ideas will contribute to either order or disorder in our inner world. This worldview will even help us not to waste hours in front of a television screen watching things which do not benefit our soul and which, later, will lead us, on many occasions, to counseling for problems that they helped to create. Television is an example, but it may be a computer, a business, a profession, or something else. We need to acquire a distinct way of thinking to the world's way of thinking, or we will never become the people whom God desires us to be.

Next, we will take a look at an exercise that someone conducted to give us an idea of how we spend our time. One week has 168 hours. Let us suppose that a long day at work is 10 hours. We sleep 7 hours, which by the way, is a good amount of time. We do not need 10 hours of sleep. Let us also suppose that our meals, added together, take up 3 hours. If we add up all of this, we come up with 20 hours per day. Monday to Friday at 5 days multiplied by 20 hours per day equals 100 hours. For Saturday and Sunday, let us suppose that we will get 8 hours of sleep each night, but we also are going to assume 3 hours for meals both Saturday and Sunday. As such, taking 3 hours to eat and 8 hours to sleep, we come up with a total of 11 hours per day. If we multiply those 11 hours by 2, we arrive at 22 hours for the weekend. So, we now have 100 hours spent from Monday to Friday plus 24 hours spent on the weekends. This gives us a total of 122 hours. If we subtract that number from the total of 168 hours in a week, we are left with 46 hours to do other things. If we multiply this number of hours by the fifty-two weeks in a year, we are left with 100 free days (99.66 to be exact). This equals a little more than three months. What did we do with all of that time?

Time goes by, and we are often most dissatisfied with how we used it. Why is that? It is because we recognize that we wasted our time. As a result, our inner world remains disorganized. We usually live in such a way that urgent matters occupy first place while we place important things in second place, and matters of priority in last place. It is common for urgent matters to be related to the demands of the workplace. Our day-to-day life looks like the following:

It is seven o'clock in the morning. We should be on our way to work and must leave no matter whether or not we have prayed or read our Bible or had the opportunity to say goodbye to our children. We have to go. Our boss is waiting for us to attend to an urgent matter.

This is everyday life for many of us. We say that God is important, but when it comes to putting this into practice, our job takes priority. After work, our priorities are relationships and commitments: birthdays, weddings, baby showers, and various other types of activities. And all the while, God occupies second place on our calendar.

Many times, I hear people say, "I feel guilty because I have not had the time this week to read my Bible, and my prayer time has all but disappeared." Nevertheless, these individuals have had the time to fulfill all of their social commitments, go to the beauty salon, get a manicure or pedicure, spend time washing their vehicles on the weekend, and so on. What is certain is that we always find a way to make time for the things that interest us. God is the one who usually has no space on our full calendar.

If we do not get our inner world in order, our priorities will never have a place in our lives. If we take a large bucket and fill it with pebbles, we will have no space for large stones. There once was a professor who performed a similar exercise in front of his students. He emptied the bucket and then filled it up with large stones. He proceeded to ask his students, "Do you think it is full?" The students affirmed that it was full. Immediately after, he started placing several small pebbles that slipped between the large stones. He asked again, "Do you think it is full?" And the students responded, "It is now, professor." He then took some sand which filled the space between the small pebbles. Once the bucket was filled with sand, the students thought that it definitely had to be at capacity, but the professor took water and poured it into the bucket, and some of the water still could fill the void between the small grains of sand. The idea behind this illustration is not to cause us to do more things in the same amount of time during the week. The lesson that this illustration teaches us is that when we place the important things first, in their rightful place, the others also find space; but the same would not be true if we inverted the order. We must do the same in our life.

Believe it or not, getting our inner world in order depends upon our relationship with God. Once we have placed God in His rightful place in our lives, we will be able to correctly prioritize our relationships with everyone else: our spouse, our children, our family members, our friends, and even our job. When our lives are in the correct order, we will usually find the space to have communion with God, and that communion depends on our peace with Him. Greater, still, is the likelihood that we will raise holy offspring for good and reap the benefits of a greater satisfaction in life.

If you want to change and start over today but do not know where to start, one way that you can determine what is important and what takes priority is to ask yourself how your relationships are going. Which ones? Well, let us start with the most important one. How is your relationship with God? If it is not going well, all of the others will not go well, and we can stop there. If we think, "My relationship with God is fine, but my relationship with my spouse is not going well," then we must continue to examine ourselves because, generally, these two things go hand in hand. The author of Proverbs tells us: "When a person's ways please the LORD, he makes even his enemies to be at peace with him" (16:7). Of course, we know that the book of Proverbs is a book of wisdom and, therefore, there are times when we do not see its sayings come to pass exactly how they are stated in their respective proverbs. Nevertheless, being a book of wisdom, it does allow us to see that, in general, things in life do happen this way.

Have you ever wondered what is the purpose of your life? The majority of people are not clear on what God's purpose is for their lives. They get up, go to work, come home exhausted, eat dinner, and then go to bed. Then, they wake up to do it all over again. We must ask ourselves what is God's purpose for our lives because, when it is not clear or obvious to us, we waste time doing things that are not part of His purpose for us.

Have you ever produced a life plan, be it a written plan or a mental plan? Frequently, our own life creates the plan while we are living it, but in reality, we must get our world in order in relation to God so that our plans can then be carried out according to His purposes. If we do not ask questions of ourselves, we will never know with certainty where we are. Have you ever asked yourself if this year there has been more of Christ's character formed in you? If the answer is yes, in which areas in particular do you believe this has occurred? This type of question helps us to understand how we are living in relation to what is important and what takes priority, because we tend to take care of urgent matters first. God, however, knows that there are things that we should tend to first. Regrettably, we frequently allow those urgent things to habitually take the place of priority things. Because of this, there is no place for God on our calendar. This is the reason why time spent in communion with God and time spent studying and meditating on the Scriptures does not fit within our everyday life, because the urgent things have continued to replace each and every one of these things. The problem is that each time we replace our priorities, the urgent things create problems. It is at that moment that our outer world is in disorder. So, our outer world becomes disarrayed because our inner world has fallen apart first.

Man's Inner and Outer World

Outer world has to do with our reputation. For many, what others think about them is more important than what God thinks about them. We may not agree with this comment, but the way we live, seeking to please others while not pleasing God, demonstrates this point. On the other hand, the outer world has to do with work, social commitments, and appearances. There are people who are highly thought of by others because they are disciplined and, therefore, very compliant. The problem is that many people who are categorized as compliant are not as compliant with God. They go to every funeral, they are in all the weddings, attend each birthday party, appear at all social functions; and now, through social media, they are able to congratulate and remain in contact with the whole world. Unfortunately, though, many of them miss the mark with God.

Inner world has to do with our character, values, and beliefs. It has to do with what we truly are and, above all, that which is related to God. We ought to be reflexive individuals if we want to cultivate our inner world. For example, we cannot simply repent without considering what that repentance implies. On one occasion, Jonathan Edwards wrote: "Lord, forgive me for the superficiality of my repentance." The greatest theologian the United States has ever produced said this. Previously, we emphasized the need for us to examine ourselves and, regarding this, Socrates, the great Greek philosopher, used to say that life is not worth living if we do not examine ourselves.

In the previous chapter we mentioned that men tend to be more task-oriented than women, and women tend to be more relationship-oriented in comparison to men. This tendency is reflected on a spiritual level as the majority of Christian women have more communion with God and pray to God more frequently than men. This is also reflected in the fact that women purchase the majority of Christian literature (70–80 percent, according to some studies); in addition, the same studies reflect that women actually read most of the Christian literature that men purchase. This task-orientated disposition causes many men to be successful in the workplace but a disaster in the family.

This reality can be illustrated by a geological phenomenon known as a sinkhole, which is a great pit or hole that suddenly opens on the surface and is capable of swallowing everything found on the surface immediately above. They owe their formation to underground changes and factors. Everything on the surface looks good up until the moment the earth gives way and collapses. The same is true with many lives that look good on the outside up until the day that the marriage or family collapses. This brings to mind an incident that took place in one of the most prestigious seminaries in the United States. One year, in particular, during the graduation ceremony there was a student who won the award for best student and received the applause of everyone in attendance. After the ceremony, while at home, his wife took a pile of books from his library, threw them on the table, and said, "Here are your books! You can marry them. I'm leaving!" This story occurred on the same day as this man's graduation from seminary, and it gives us an idea of the existence of things that are capable of corroding the interior of a person, a relationship, a marriage, or a family. This occurs because priorities have not been clearly defined and, although they may have been put into words, they have not been put into practice.

We must remember that our priorities are related to our purpose in life. The order of our priorities determines how we will live while also determining the problems that can be created. Let us take a look at another illustration so that we can better understand the way in which the order of priorities influences these things. There exists a thesis known as the Pareto principle, which many people have applied to several different areas. The Pareto principle is also known as the 80/20 rule. In one of its applications, it may be said that 20 percent of the defects affect 80 percent of the processes. In a company that manufactures multiple different products, some would say that, based on the principle, 20 percent of said products probably generate 80 percent of revenues. We could apply this principle in another way: 20 percent of this book will surely produce 80 percent of the impact upon its readers or 20 percent of a sermon will produce 80 percent of the impact upon those who listen to it. This is not an absolute principle, but it does give us an idea of what Pareto was trying to illustrate.

Similarly, we could say that if we organize our life in such a way that the first 20 percent of our priorities are made up of God and our family, perhaps we could avoid 80 percent of the negative consequences that we might reap in life. To put it another way, if the first 20 percent of our priorities revolve around work, social commitments, and friendships instead of God and our family, this disorder in our inner world, therefore, is the cause of 80 percent of the problems that we have: personal conflicts; marital conflicts; problems with our children; moral, ethical, spiritual, financial, and health problems, etc. Perhaps one of the most common problems among Christians is financial difficulties and, in the majority of cases, they are not primarily financial in nature; rather, they have to do with our *being*, that is how we live and how we see life and the world. Our concept of the role of money determines how we spend it and how we waste it. In the financial realm, there are expenses that we should not incur because we do not have the money to do so, and if we do not have the money to spend, we cannot spend it. You may use your credit card, but even with that, you eventually have to pay back that debt with added interest. The problems that we reap are the interest that we pay for the things that we did not prioritize well. This disorder is produced in the interior of the individual before being produced on the exterior.

Decision-Making

When it comes time to make decisions, we must remember the Christian premise that every decision has a spiritual dimension. For example, a church or ministry should have a budget. Yet, if the budget is the only criterion or the most important criterion used to determine the expenditures of a church, then God has been displaced from His rightful place. He should be the key player who determines how we see life, how we react to it, how we spend money, and how we manage it. Within God's parameters exists a budget, which allows us not to waste the resources that He has entrusted to us. The master of the budget is God, and this is a principle that we must remember. We should not buy something simply because we have the money to buy it, because if we act this way, God has been replaced. He is the owner of all the silver and gold. Therefore, when it comes time to make a purchase, God should be the one who guides us to either make the purchase or wait and save our money.

The Christian premise is that every decision has a spiritual dimension. Since all creation belongs to God, then every decision must have a spiritual dimension. If this is true (and we believe that it is), our prayer life will be indispensable. The Word of God will be the same because it is His Word which informs our worldview. On the other hand, prayer is the vehicle through which God will continue to move us in one direction or another.

In his book *The Man in the Mirror*, Patrick Morley indicates that decisions can have either a priority aspect or a moral aspect. The priority aspect oftentimes has to do with what is good, best, and excellent.[4] The moral aspect has to do with what is right and wrong. The monthly rent payment may be a priority for the family, but the monthly rent for a luxury home may have a moral component if the family's income is not enough to support the rent or if the intention of renting such a home is purely materialistic. Do not get caught up in prestige, the pursuit of money, growth, or merit. We live trapped by these things, and they condition us as to whether or not we see ourselves as citizens of another world or another realm. We must see ourselves as exiles, as John Piper states in the sermon we quoted at the beginning of this chapter. While we get our inner world in order, we have to learn to make moral decisions and priority decisions at the same time.

On the other hand, many times, knowing how to wait is the right decision. If someone were to ask me what is the best thing that I have ever done in my life, I would not say that it is preaching, teaching, or counseling. I believe that the best thing I have ever done in life is waiting. God has taught me to wait and, in waiting, I have avoided making many bad decisions. God has saved me a lot of time, strength, energy, and even money. Some have said to me, "Pastor, I made this decision because I had to do something," and I always have the same response: "Waiting on the Lord and His timing is doing something."

Some people who know us well have asked us how we are able to accomplish so many tasks and, with all sincerity, the best answer we can give has to do with decision-making and the correct use of our time in order not to waste it. There are many things that, quite frankly, are a total waste of time. We always strive to use our time well because this is what determines how efficient we are. There are many conversations that are purely trivial; and although there is a time for them, they should not take up a lot of our time. We cannot dedicate a large portion of our time to trivial things. For if we did, we would simply be wasting it. Paul writes to Timothy with the following recommendation: "Timothy, guard what has been entrusted to you, avoiding irreverent and empty speech . . ." (1 Tim. 6:20a). And in his second letter to Timothy, he repeats something similar: "Avoid irreverent and empty speech, since those who engage in it will produce even more godlessness" (2 Tim. 2:16). It is necessary to have substantial conversations that feed us, help us, teach us, and edify us. And when appropriate, there is a time for joking and laughter. There are even some who, apart from the exchange of necessary information for everyday life, spend day after day discussing only the most superficial things in life. This is not a wise investment of our time.

Delegating Tasks in Order to Organize Our World

This is an area that has been difficult and demands improvement. If you have more things on your plate than you can actually do, perhaps you are trying to accomplish things which God has not called you to accomplish. Think about delegating some of them. Having more things on our plate than we can handle is something that has certainly happened to us on a personal level, and perhaps we continue to experience this. If there is one thing we know, it is that God certainly understands that we have twenty-four hours in a day, and He will not ask us to do things that require thirty hours a day to accomplish because that is not the God we know. So, sometimes we have things on our plate that God has not placed there, and we must eliminate them. On occasion, the solution is to delegate. There are tasks that must be delegated because others can do them better or because we need to dedicate our time to the things that only we can do. A lot of times, we tend to do things ourselves because we think that others will not do them as well as we would or because we think that if we delegate them to someone else, it will take longer. Sometimes this occurs only at the beginning, because later the individual to whom we have delegated the task will have learned to do it well, making better use of his time. The final answer is not to pack more things in our day but to be able to do those tasks which truly correspond to our function or role.

It really stands out that when Jethro, Moses' father-in-law, visited him, the first thing that he noticed was that this great leader needed to delegate responsibilities. Let us take a look at the story and then make a couple of observations:

> The next day Moses sat down to judge the people, and they stood around Moses from morning until evening. When Moses' father-in-law saw everything he was doing for them he asked, "What is this you're doing for the people? Why are you alone sitting as judge, while all the people stand around you from morning until evening?"
>
> Moses replied to his father-in-law, "Because the people come to me to inquire of God. Whenever they have a dispute, it comes to me, and I make a decision between one man and another. I teach them God's statutes and laws."
>
> "What you're doing is not good," Moses' father-in-law said to him. "You will certainly

> wear out both yourself and these people who are
> with you, because the task is too heavy for you.
> You can't do it alone. Now listen to me; I will
> give you some advice, and God be with you. You
> be the one to represent the people before God
> and bring their cases to him. Instruct them about
> the statutes and laws, and teach them the way to
> live and what they must do. But you should select
> from all the people able men, God-fearing, trust-
> worthy, and hating dishonest profit. Place them
> over the people as commanders of thousands,
> hundreds, fifties, and tens. They should judge
> the people at all times. Then they can bring you
> every major case but judge every minor case
> themselves. In this way you will lighten your
> load, and they will bear it with you." (Exod.
> 18:13–22)

Moses had not considered the fact that some cases did not require his wisdom and expertise, as there were others who could be responsible for these cases so that he could deal with the more complex ones. This would free up some of his time to do the things that only he could do. This is the art of delega-tion. Later, when Moses complains to God about the burden of the people upon him, God asks him to gather seventy elders of Israel in order to help him bear the burden (Num. 11:16–18). Suddenly, the leadership of the people passed from one person (Moses) to seventy. Do you think Moses had to learn to delegate? This example makes us feel better when we have not been good at delegating.

Jethro's recommendations were important; so much so, that we need to point out a few of them:

- Moses had to delegate. If not, he would have
  run the risk of collapsing, as he was about to
  occur according to the account of Numbers 11.

- Moses had to dedicate time to teach those to whom he had delegated tasks: "Instruct them about the statutes and laws, and teach them the way to live and what they must do" (Exod. 18:20).
- In order to delegate well, we need a good group of individuals to do the job: "But you should select . . . able men, God-fearing, trustworthy, and hating dishonest profit" (Exod. 18:21a).

Some of us simply do not know how to delegate, so it is good to pause and reflect upon some of the things that make it difficult for us to do so. In the previous chapter, we saw some of these characteristics. Among them are:

1. **Perfectionism.** We think that no one will do things like we do them. That may be true, but if we do not learn to delegate, our organization or ministry will soon become stagnant in its growth and will not be effective because all of these decisions must be made by the same person.
2. **Insecurity.** Our insecurities lead us to distrust others. One of the benefits of delegating is that it increases team morale and the trust that our team members feel has been placed in them. In the meantime, you will be less burned and will have more time to attend to vital matters.
3. **Fear of losing authority.** We are likely fearful that by delegating we may lose the power to decide at any moment, but authority is something totally different. Authority has to do with the respect that others have of you as a result of your good performance and the consistency between your words and actions.

The reasons why we often fail to delegate are related to our inner world; hence, the importance of examining them.

Final Reflection

Why dedicate so much time to the topic of delegating in a chapter that deals with getting our inner world in order? Because, if we do not delegate, many times our world falls into disorder, and we find ourselves on the verge of collapse. Notice how Moses practically arrived at this point:

> So Moses asked the LORD, "Why have you brought such trouble on your servant? Why are you angry with me, and why do you burden me with all these people? Did I conceive all these people? Did I give them birth so you should tell me, 'Carry them at your breast, as a nursing mother carries a baby,' to the land that you swore to give their ancestors? Where can I get meat to give all these people? For they are weeping to me, 'Give us meat to eat!' I can't carry all these people by myself. They are too much for me. If you are going to treat me like this, please kill me right now if I have found favor with you, and don't let me see my misery anymore." (Num. 11:11–15)

Moses was angry at God due to fatigue produced by a lot of work but also due to the continual complaints of the people. We can see this if we read the previous verses in this passage. God's response was not to order the people not to complain, as that was not going to happen due to the sinful nature of man. God's response was to delegate Moses' work to seventy men . . . not three or seven or ten, but seventy. That is incredible. If God had not solved this problem, both the inner world and outer world of Moses would have suffered the consequences. But God in His mercy intervened and helped Moses where he needed it. This is a great story with great lessons for us.

Delegating also allows us to devote more time to organizing our priorities, which is where we began. The team that forms around us can also help us to make decisions, which is another area that we addressed in this chapter. All of this will help us get both our inner and outer world in order.

CHAPTER 3

Be a Biblically Minded Servant

For as he thinks within himself, so he is.
Proverbs 23:7a NASB

No one recalls.
Isaiah 44:19a NASB

Introduction

Perhaps one of the features which Christians who attend biblically sound churches would find striking is the lack of a biblical mind. This comes up in their daily conversations, in their lifestyles, in the way they dress, in how they spend their money, in the way they debate issues, in the way they treat others whom they consider inferior to them, and in all other areas of their lives. According to the Barna Research Group, fewer than 50 percent of Americans are able to name the four Gospels, and some 60 percent are not able to recite five of the Ten Commandments. Around 50 percent of high school seniors surveyed said that Sodom and Gomorrah were husband and wife, while a considerable number of those surveyed indicated that Billy Graham preached the Sermon on the Mount.[1] We may find these statistics laughable; however, in my opinion, I do not believe that biblical knowledge in Latin America, the region in which I live and minister, is very different.

In 1994, the US historian Mark Noll published a book titled *The Scandal of the Evangelical Mind*, which opens with the following phrase: "The scandal of the evangelical mind is that there is not much of an evangelical mind."[2] The author continues by asking why it is that those evangelicals who enjoy financial resources, status, and influence have contributed so little to the academic world.

The absence of a biblical mind makes spiritual discernment impossible, something which brings consequences to the individual and to the people of God in general. At one point in the history of the Hebrew people, God said the following through the prophet Isaiah: "Therefore My people go into exile for their lack of knowledge; And their honorable men are famished, and their multitude is parched with thirst" (Isa. 5:13 NASB). God's people were taken into exile due to their multiple sinful acts, but God attributed their behavior to a lack of a biblical mind in them, something the text that we just read describes as a lack of discernment. It is impossible for man to acquire true wisdom without first knowing God. It is precisely the knowledge of God that allows us to know things about ourselves so that we can then know the rest of what we need to know. The great theologian John Calvin begins his famous work, *Institutes of the Christian Religion* with this idea:

> Nearly all the wisdom we possess, that is to say, true and sound wisdom, consists of two parts: the knowledge of God and ourselves. [. . .] Again, it is certain that man never achieves a clear knowledge of himself unless he has first looked upon

God's face, and then descends from contemplating him to scrutinize himself.[3]

Here, Calvin allows us to see that the man who does not examine the Word of God will not be able to acquire a biblical mind because everything begins with the knowledge of God, and it is precisely in the Scriptures where He best reveals Himself to human beings. There is a limited knowledge of God which everyone can access by observing creation, while another part of that knowledge has been embodied in the conscience of every human being by the work of God, just as the apostle explains in Romans 1:19–20.

The Fall's Impact on the Mind

God created man (the good); man disobeyed (the bad); God decided to redeem him (the new) in order to ultimately glorify him (the perfect).[4] We currently still find ourselves in the process of redemption, through which God seeks to restore all that was damaged by the Fall. But in the meantime, it is necessary for us to comprehend how the Fall affected humankind. The Word of God uses different adjectives to refer to the fallen mind when it speaks of:

- A hardened mind (2 Cor. 3:14)
- A blinded mind (2 Cor. 4:4)
- A futile mind (Eph. 4:17)
- A darkened understanding (Eph. 4:18)
- An unspiritual mind (Col. 2:18)
- A depraved mind (1 Tim. 6:5)
- A hardened heart (Mark 6:52)

The fall of man was so deep that the apostle Paul later points out that "the person without the Spirit does not receive what comes from God's Spirit, because it is foolishness to him; he is not able to understand it since it is evaluated spiritually" (1 Cor. 2:14).

Martin Luther understood perfectly just how profound the impact of the Fall was, which is why he wrote the following:

> Due to original sin, our nature is so curved in upon itself at its deepest levels that it not only bends the best gifts of God toward itself in order to enjoy them (as the moralists and hypocrites make evident), nay, rather, "uses" God in order to obtain them, but it does not even know that, in this wicked, twisted, crooked way, it seeks everything, including God, only for itself.[5]

With these words, Martin Luther helps us to see that the fallen mind produces in all of us an entirely self-centered way of thinking and living. Adam lost his vertical orientation (toward God), which he naturally possessed. After the Fall, his orientation was mostly toward himself. This is why, during the Age of Enlightenment, man strongly affirmed that the human being is the measure of all things, which should not surprise us, given the corruption of the human mind. John Calvin, one of the great Reformers and, without a doubt, one of the greatest theologians in the history of the church, made the following comment regarding our corruption:

> This perversity never ceases but constantly produces new fruits, in other words, those works of the flesh which we formerly described, just as a lighted furnace sends forth sparks and flames, or a fountain without ceasing pours out water . . . For our nature is not only utterly devoid of goodness, but so prolific in all kinds of evil that it can never be idle . . . everything which is in man, from the intellect to the will, from the soul even to the flesh is defiled and pervaded with this concupiscence.[6]

This is the reason why Calvin spoke of the total depravity of man, teaching that each and every one of our human faculties has been stained by sin. The depraved mind reasons in the following way:

- **We are what we think we are.** Therefore, our titles and achievements give us identity.
- **We do bad things, but we are not bad people.** Others judge us unjustly.
- **If something goes wrong, it is not our fault.** Eve and the serpent in the garden of Eden are evidence of this.
- **Morality is relative.** But when someone sins against us, it is clear that this principle is violated.

All of this allows us to see the great need of cultivating a biblical mind.

The Importance of a Biblical Mind

At the beginning of the twentieth century, we witnessed a growth in the fundamentalist movement, which saw itself threatened by the questioning of biblical authority by those within the movement associated with liberal theology. Sadly, many fundamentalists began to develop a certain suspicion concerning everything that had to do with the intellect, as if faith and reason were opposites, when in reality, in the mind of God, both are connected to His revelation. If God created the world, as He truly did, He created man in His image and likeness; and after He revealed himself to man, it is logical to conclude that He hoped that by reasoning we could understand His revelation and, upon understanding it, we would develop a genuine and biblical faith.

In his epistle to the Romans, the apostle Paul helps us see part of what we are trying to explain: "Do not be conformed to this age, but be transformed by the renewing of your mind, so that you may discern what is the good, pleasing, and perfect will of God" (Rom. 12:2). This text tells us clearly that by means of our mind we must resist conforming to this world, something that the Holy Spirit will help us to do. At the same time, we must renew our mind (with the Word of God) in order to be transformed. It is impossible to experience a transformation of life if our mind has not first been transformed.

The mind is the operations center that directs our thoughts, emotions, decisions, and actions. We think first, then we feel, and we finally make a mental decision which leads us to putting the action into practice. The role of the mind in the Christian life is revealed in different ways in the Word of God. In Matthew 22:37 we read the following: "He said to him, 'Love the Lord your God with all your heart, with all your soul, and with all your mind.'" Our mind is what allows us to understand what God has revealed and, therefore, it helps us to understand it, also.

How the Mind Is Formed or Deformed

We mentioned how the apostle Paul instructs us in Romans 12:2, telling us that we should not adapt to the currents of the world that deform our mind. Rather, we should be transformed by the renewal of our mind in order to see the formation of a biblical mind, something to which we have already alluded. Each auditory and visual stimulus that we experience leaves a trace or memory in the mind. The world continuously bombards us with its ideas, and if we do not have a capable filter and something that we can use to counter such a bombardment, the mind will take on a form of its own. Our strategy to combat the patterns of this age should be offensive and not simply defensive. We must prepare an intentional attack which renews our mind by the Truth of God. Paul alluded to this in his Second Letter to the Corinthians when he wrote:

> [S]ince the weapons of our warfare are not of the flesh, but are powerful through God for the demolition of strongholds. We demolish arguments and every proud thing that is raised up against the knowledge of God, and we take every thought captive to obey Christ. (2 Cor. 10:4–5)

The idea behind this text is that the Christian should compare everything we learn against the biblical standard and then reject all that which is not consistent with the revelation of God while obeying His Word even when the world rejects and does not understand Him. If we allow our mind to be frequently exposed to things or situations that go against our values, be it by what we read or what we watch, we will undoubtedly become desensitized and will increasingly accept greater levels of sin. If we have already been exposed to such anti-values while discovering that we have been desensitized, the correct decision is for us to separate ourselves from the source of sin which has desensitized us so that we can allow our hardened conscience to become sensitive again. We have to replace all of the bad that we have learned with values found in the kingdom of heaven. Society tends to judge something as good when, in reality, it is bad; while qualifying something as bad when, in reality, it is good. This is not a new problem; rather, it started in the garden of Eden when Adam listened to the voice of the serpent (which was bad) and ignored the voice of God (the only thing that was good). During the time of the prophet Isaiah, God pronounced an oracle of woe upon His own people when He said, "Woe to those who call evil good and good evil, who substitute darkness for light and light for darkness, who substitute bitter for sweet and sweet for bitter" (Isa. 5:20). The little word *woe* foretells judgment from God.

The substitution of anti-values with biblical values is vitally important because the mind thinks according to values which accumulate over time. What we should ask ourselves is: "What is a value?" A value is something that has merit, meaning, or significance for us and leads us to react or behave in a determined manner. Our values give birth to our emotions, our feelings, our desires, our habits, and our behavioral patterns. Some prefer to use the term *virtue* because they understand it to be more in line with what the Bible reveals. This prevents someone from referring to a certain concept, however distorted it may be, and saying that, for him, it is a value. There certainly has been a massive loss of Christian values in our day. We have lost the sense of shame, the sense of duty, and the sense of guilt. It is impossible for a society to adequately function when these three values are absent. If you want to see what a society that has lost these values looks like, all you have to do is read the daily newspaper or the epistle of Paul to the Romans, specifically Romans 1:18–32.

Factors that Contribute to the Formation of Our Values

On one occasion Francis Schaeffer said that "our values are things that we have collected unthinkingly, like germs from life's streets, ever since we were born." This is very true. Man tends to take his values from his idols or from the individuals whom he admires. The old man accumulates values according to the flesh (Eph. 2:3), but the new man must study the Word in order to obtain his values from the revelation of God. Values form the standard through which a person judges, measures, compares, and lives. Changing our values is difficult because it means no longer being what we once were, and this terrifies people. Additionally, we do not typically find it easy to change our values due to the source from which we got them:

1. Family
2. Secular and Christian Education
3. Friends
4. Culture
5. Books
6. Media
7. Music, art, drama (movies, TV shows, etc.)

We often accept what our family teaches us without even questioning it; we accept as intelligent what secular education promotes; and we receive as fashionable what our friends pass along to us. The things that we learn from culture form part of our identity because culture tends to form us. Music is a good instrument for transmitting values, for better or worse. It has been said that we were created to filter our experiences through our conscience. But the values that music transmits often are capable of dodging our conscience, reaching the brain and changing our forms of behavior.

Many of the world's own values are absorbed by our mind as if by osmosis or subconsciously. However, new values must be formed intentionally. When we come to Christ, we must examine our values, or else we will continue to think and live as we did before. Our old values can be compared to a time bomb that explodes when we least expect it; because of this, we have an important need to exchange them for the values of the new man. The Word of God speaks of this exchange in Ephesians 4:22–24:

> [T]o take off your former way of life, the old self that is corrupted by deceitful desires, to be renewed in the spirit of your minds, and to put on the new self, the one created according to God's likeness in righteousness and purity of the truth.

Obstacles to the Christian Mind

I. Distraction

While describing the effects of the Fall upon the human mind, Albert Mohler states that we all have "theological attention deficit disorder."[7] This helps us understand that each of us is easily distracted by what occurs around us. Thus, we frequently end up knowing many things that do not interest God all while not knowing many things that interest our Creator and Redeemer.

When Jesus announced that He must go to Jerusalem and suffer much at the hands of the Jewish authorities, Peter interrupted Him and exclaimed: "'Oh no, Lord! This will never happen to you!' Jesus turned and told Peter, 'Get behind me, Satan! You are a hindrance to me because you are not thinking about God's concerns but human concerns'" (Matt. 16:22b–23). This is typically our problem: in our everyday lives we give importance to the things of man before the things of God. We easily lose interest in the things of the kingdom of heaven in order to place such interest in the things of the world. We become easily distracted by the banalities of life and many even lose interest when they are not the center of attention of whatever is occurring.

2. Prejudice

All human beings, in one way or another, have prejudices. Some are theological and do not allow us to understand positions contrary to our own; others are philosophical in nature and make it impossible for us to understand (although we do not accept it) a different worldview than ours. Other prejudices are cultural and cause us to reject anything culturally different than that with which we were raised; and while we have prejudices against certain ways of being and get along extremely well with certain people, there are others who, quite frankly, irritate us. Nathanael expressed a cultural prejudice against Jesus when he said, "Can anything good come out of Nazareth?" (John 1:46a). The Jews had racial and religious prejudices against the Gentiles and, therefore, severely condemned them.

3. Pride

Human pride is manifested in different ways, different moments, and different places. We frequently assume that we know what others do not know, without even having analyzed what we think we do know. Other times, we assume that we could do something better than someone else, without having done it before. This is like the person who has never planted a church but is sure that if he did plant a church, he would do it better than the majority of the people who have actually planted one. We assume the position of judge and accuse others of the same things of which we are guilty. This pride grows when we possess some level of knowledge because, as Paul so well says in 1 Corinthians 8:1, "knowledge puffs up."

Distinguishing Marks of a Biblical Mind[8]

It reasons from an eternal perspective.

The way in which we perceive life events determines how we react to them. Sadly, much of what we see corresponds more to the condition of our heart than to reality itself. When the disciples who were in the boat in the midst of the storm saw Jesus walking on the water, they concluded that what they were seeing was a ghost, although such was not the case. On this occasion, two factors combined to give them an incorrect perception:

1. A pagan worldview which led them to believe in ghosts.
2. Their lack of faith to believe that Jesus was able to walk on the water.

After his conversion, Paul's way of judging others changed completely; because of this, he expresses the following as he writes to the Corinthians:

> From now on, then, we do not know anyone from a worldly perspective. Even if we have known Christ from a worldly perspective, yet now we no longer know him in this way. Therefore, if anyone is in Christ, he is a new creation; the old has passed away, and see, the new has come! (2 Cor. 5:16–17)

This teaching allows us to see that there are two ways of evaluating life:

1. "From a worldly perspective," which corresponds to the old man's way of thinking.
2. "From the Holy Spirit's perspective," which corresponds to the new man, the new creation in Christ.

Before his conversion, perhaps for Paul, a client was someone to be taken advantage of; a woman could be someone with whom to have children or gain pleasure; a Christian was someone to persecute. After his conversion, Paul did not view anyone according to the flesh, but as potential converts to the Lord. This serves to illustrate that what we are determines how we see things. There exists a perspective both above the sun and under the sun, as King Solomon indicates in the book of Ecclesiastes. The perspective under the sun led Solomon to consider that all life was burdensome and meaningless, and this left him completely empty. Unfortunately, this is how a large portion of humanity lives.

It thinks in terms of community and not individualistically.

The fallen mind always tends to think in a self-centered way; but as He redeems it, God begins to help us to think more in terms of community. If this has been important before, it is even more important in the midst of a generation as narcissistic as ours. In the first century, people tended to think collectively. As such, if someone in a small community received a visitor, the entire community, in a way, considered that the visitor was the responsibility of everyone. In chapters 2 and 4 of the book of Acts, we see how the church responded as a united community, even to an extreme such that some sold all that they had in order to provide for the needs of others. The text says that they "held all things in common" (Acts 2:44). Later we read: "Now the entire group of those who believed were of one heart and mind, and no one claimed that any of his possessions was his own, but instead they held everything in common" (4:32). This is possible only when the Spirit of God is working in us.

It submits to authority, beginning with God and His Word.

By nature, the fallen man is rebellious and has a sense of autonomy. Both of these can be seen in small children who want to get their way. As we have observed, we do not have to teach a small child how to disobey because it comes naturally to him. The continuous struggle we have is to teach this defenseless creature how to obey the ones who brought him into the world and then everyone else who has authority over him. If obedience is difficult even for those who have been born again, we only have to imagine how difficult it is for those who neither love God nor His revelation. Sin is nothing more than a creature's cry of independence, and this began in the garden of Eden. In reality, we could say that it began in heaven when Lucifer wanted to be like God. It would seem that the creature does not yet tolerate having to submit to authority; this is another conclusion at which we arrive simply by observing the behavior of a child.

It values the dignity of life.

Ever since the United States legalized abortion in 1973, we have been struggling worldwide for the dignity of life. The only reason for this continued struggle is that human beings have lost all respect for the image of God impressed upon them. With the passing of time, the legalization of abortion prepared the way for the legalization of euthanasia in some nations of the world. When we lose respect for the most defenseless members of society, we do not respect anyone else. Shortly after the Fall of Adam and Eve, we see how Cain murdered his brother, Abel (Gen. 4). In Genesis 9:6, God sees the need to introduce the death penalty as a way of protecting the human race. Nations, which once inherited a Christian worldview in certain areas, presently have begun to get rid of the death penalty for murder as they have lost the value of the dignity of life. God introduced such a severe penalty precisely because of the high regard that He has of His image in each and every human being, something that men and women today do not have, which is why they find the death penalty horrifying for those who have taken the life of another human being.

It values the revelation of God.

A non-Christian mind has neither an appreciation for the Word of God nor an appreciation for what God thinks about the decisions it makes. Therefore, we could say that the person who does not know God makes decisions based on the information he has, as well as reason and experience. This unleashed the two great world wars among other conflicts at a global level. But the truly Christian mind orders thoughts in another way. It takes the information that it receives and filters the information through the conscience and, even more so, through the revelation of God. And later, through the power of the grace of God, it takes every captive thought to the feet of Jesus, arriving at a final decision.

The Loss of the Christian Mind

For years, Americans have debated whether or not the United States was ever a Christian nation. Opinions are divided, but we believe that there is a great consensus that the USA was at least greatly impacted by Christian values at some point in its history. To some extent, this impact gave the American society a Christian conscience, which led to many of their laws being consistent with the revelation of God. Since the 1960s, these laws have continued to change, and along with these changes, the loss of the Christian mind has become even greater. Some may find it strange that I refer to the United States, as I am a Latino who ministers in Latin America, but the reasons why are quite simple. On the one hand, since the Second World War, the United States has been the power which has most influenced the world, something that is also true with relation to the expansion of the Christian faith. For many years, no other nation has sent so many missionaries beyond its borders. On the other hand, as the Protestant Reformation never truly arrived at our shores in Latin America, we have not seen an impact at a national level such as occurred in Europe after the Reformation and later in the United States. Regarding this, let us turn our attention to a few details concerning the legacy left by the Puritans in the United States.

Cotton Mather (1663–1728), one of the best-known Puritans, said, "Ignorance is the mother not of devotion but heresy." This way of thinking contributed to many Puritans being highly educated. It is worth mentioning some of the characteristics common among them:

- They founded universities.
- Their children learned to read and write before six years of age.
- They studied art, science, philosophy, and many other branches of knowledge as a way of loving God with their minds.
- The Puritan minister was considered a spiritual and intellectual authority in the community.[9]

Sadly, this loss of the Christian mind began well before the year 1960. In the eighteenth century, two very influential philosophers began a ferocious attack on Christianity. The Bible began to be seen as an ethical guide. From the mid-eighteenth century to the beginning of the twentieth century, the German Higher Criticism movement severely questioned the authority of the Scripture and began to question its authorship, its date of writing, the origin of each book of the Bible, and so on. Ultimately, the result was that almost everything that up to that point had been commonly agreed upon among biblical scholars began to be questioned. The church's response was a massive retreat from society, and evangelicals began founding their own schools and universities and, over time, founded their own radio and television stations. This movement by the church was known as fundamentalism. With this movement, society lost the salt and light of the world; it lost us as representatives of Christ.[10]

J. P. Moreland comments: "This withdrawal and marginalization of the church has had devastating consequences for our attempt to produce vibrant, confident disciples and to penetrate our culture with a Christian worldview and the gospel of Christ."[11]

The Higher Criticism movement had consequences for the church. It gave rise to a movement that was suspicious of everything that might sound or look intellectual, rational, or contrary to faith. Therefore, there arose a poor interpretation of the relationship between faith and reason. Those on the most extreme of the pendulum did not even want their children to study at universities because they considered education to be completely secular. Others considered seminary education to be dangerous to the Christian life, something from which we have yet to recover. To be sure, many seminaries of liberal persuasion have contributed to damaging the faith of many, and others of orthodox persuasion have produced more scholars than godly men. But the answer is not to condemn seminary education, but rather to correct that which has been twisted. Many have misrepresented the Bible, but that should not cause us to abandon it, rather to denounce what is wrong and rectify the errors. We can say the same of seminary education. Another group reacted by producing a more emotional faith, as well as a more superficial understanding of the Christian faith. Such is true of a large number of Christians in Latin America. During the time of Jesus, the Essenes were an aloof community who lived around the Dead Sea in order to withdraw from society and avoid corruption. They produced the famous documents found in the caves of Qumran. Later, perhaps beginning around the fourth to fifth century, a monastic movement began, which led its members, the monks, to withdraw to remote places in order to dedicate themselves to a life of contemplation and study. Nevertheless,

Jesus, Paul, the Reformers, and the Puritans remained a part of the society because they understood their work of being the salt of the earth and the light of the world. No one expressed it better than Jesus Himself in the Sermon on the Mount:

> "You are the light of the world. A city situated on a hill cannot be hidden. No one lights a lamp and puts it under a basket, but rather on a lampstand, and it gives light for all who are in the house. In the same way, let your light shine before others, so that they may see your good works and give glory to your Father in heaven." (Matt. 5:14–16)

In our day, we also see that many Christians erroneously separate the sacred from the secular. Certainly, before the Protestant Reformation, there existed a clear division between the layperson and the person ordained for ministry work. This caused a wide division between these two worlds. Luther, like the other Reformers, emphasized the doctrine known as the priesthood of all believers. They understood that all believers had a vocation to which they had been called by God and from which they were to serve Him. Therefore, it is wrong for the Christian minister to feel superior to the individual who carries out his function as a layperson. For the Christian, the whole life is sacred because, as the Reformers understood so well, we live *Coram Deo*, which means that our whole life is lived before the face of God. The words of J. P. Moreland help us to understand this point even better:

> But for a disciple, the purpose of college is not just to get a job. Rather, it is to discover a vocation, to identify a field of study in and through which I can serve Christ as my Lord. And one way to serve Him in this way is to learn to think in a Christian manner about my major. A person's Christianity doesn't begin at a dorm Bible

study, when class is over; it permeates all of one's
life, including how one thinks about the ideas in
one's college major.[12]

Another consequence of the loss of the Christian mind is the
privatization of the faith. For many, Christianity is a uniform that
they put on for church each Sunday, only not to wear it the rest of
the week. We can think of an occasion on which a Christian has
told us that he does not wish to identify himself as a Christian at
the office because others will point out when he does not behave
like one. This reveals a serious problem regarding how we understand our faith. First, the most important thing is not that others
would point out our behavior, but rather that God would be the
one who continually points it out. Second, if your colleagues at
work are unable to notice that there is something in you that
distinguishes you from everyone else, perhaps there truly does
not exist anything distinct within you; and this is something even
more serious because we would be talking about someone who
thinks he is a Christian even though he is not.

Final Reflection

A biblical mind requires a self-evaluation in which we ask
ourselves: With what are we filling our mind? On what are
we focusing our mental energy? What are the sources of our
meditation?

Knowledge has been classified in different ways since the
time of Aristotle. For the purpose of our study, we will use the
following classification of knowledge:

Knowledge is information.

Perspective is wisdom.

Conviction is certainty.

Character is doing "good" things naturally.

Ability is the set of our habits.

Many people have information (**knowledge**), but they do not know how to apply it (**wisdom**). Therefore, there is no consistency in their walk (**conviction**). As a consequence, they never even partially display the image of Christ (**character**), which is the natural way of living (**habits**).

Let us remember that it is possible for us to memorize the Bible without knowing it. We can know facts about it without understanding its content, and we truly cannot come to know something until we make it a practice.

CHAPTER 4

Be a Set-Apart Servant

But as the one who called you is holy, you
also are to be holy in all your conduct; for it
is written, Be holy, because I am holy.

1 Peter 1:15–16

Introduction

The holiness of God is the attribute which places Him in an exclusive category; it separates Him both from inanimate creation and any other living thing. Undoubtedly, there are other attributes of God which no other being possesses, but His holiness is that one attribute that makes it impossible for anyone to see His face and live. The seraphim who were created to minister in His presence have the awareness to cover their faces, just as the prophet Isaiah indicates in chapter 6 of the book which bears his name. No other attribute of God is repeated three times, as occurs with His holiness. Both Isaiah 6:3 in the Old Testament and Revelation 4:8 in the New Testament emphatically state that God is "holy, holy, holy." In Hebrew, repetition was one of the devices used to emphasize certain things, similar to how we now underline a particular text, place it in bold letters, or perhaps even highlight it so that it stands out. But the Hebrew people repeated ideas so that they would stand out. As we said before, no other attribute of God is repeated even two times in the biblical account, much less three times. The holiness of God is intrinsic to His being, whereas ours is the result, in the first place, of the sacrifice of Christ on our behalf that He grants to us, while later it is the fruit of God's work in us through the process of sanctification.

Such sanctification is the work of the Spirit of God, but unlike salvation, which is an exclusive work of our God (monergism), it is a synergism through which God, by means of His grace, urges us to actively participate in our sanctification. God is the author of both our salvation and sanctification. But in salvation, man has no participation. He is only the receiver of the gift and, because of this, there are no believers who are any more saved than others. All of us enjoy the same salvation. Nevertheless, when we speak of sanctification, we do find those who are more sanctified than others not only because of how long they have been in the faith, but also because, while some have been diligent in working on their sanctification, others have been lazy. Sanctification is not produced by a process of osmosis, rather by means of our exposure to the means of grace used by God. When we decide to study the Word, we reflect on its teachings, gain insight, and apply it; on the contrary, when we decide not to do any of these things, we are contributing to or opposing the process of sanctification which God has begun in our lives. In the verse from the First Letter of Peter that we quoted above, we see that God did not exhort us to behave in a holy manner; rather, that we be holy. And in this command, we can again observe the principle of "being before doing."

The Servant of God Is a "Set-Apart" Person

In Hebrew, there are two primary meanings of the word *holy*. The first of the two is *kodesh*, which means "separate." In the majority of cases throughout redemptive history, when God called someone to serve Him, He called him out from his environment, from a place of corruption, in order to take him to a place where he could be cleansed. God calls Abraham and says to him: "Go from your land, your relatives, and your father's house to the land that I will show you" (Gen. 12:1). Up until this moment, Abraham lived together with his father in a land that worshiped pagan Gods (Josh. 24:2). Then, when God began to work in him, He called him out of his pagan background and set him apart from his family and land. In order to walk with God, we must set ourselves apart because we cannot walk with God while continuing in the same direction in which we were previously going.

The same occurred with the nation of Israel. God led them into the desert, thus separating them from the pagan world, from the false gods of Egypt, from idolatry and immorality, to form a holy nation unto Himself. In the New Testament, God follows the same pattern. The word *church* comes from the Greek word *ekklesia* (from *ek*, "out of," and *klesis*, "call"; from *kaleo*, "to call").[1] We have been called to leave the world behind. This is what Paul instructs the Corinthians to do: "Therefore, *come out from among them and be separate*, says the Lord; *do not touch any unclean thing*, and I will welcome you" (2 Cor. 6:17, emphasis added). The phrase "come out from among them" has nothing to do with our being better, but with the fact that if we remain there our flesh will be seduced by the attractions of the world, and we will return to the place out of which the Lord brought us. Leaders must model this life of separation.

The book of Leviticus has been called the book of the priests. In this book, God highlights the holiness of His being so that the Levites or spiritual leaders of the people never forget the important need to model for the people that which honors God and that which the people need to see in their leaders: holiness. In Leviticus 11:45, God reminds the people how He brought them out of the land of slavery and pagan immorality: "For I am the LORD, who brought you up from the land of Egypt to be your God, so you must be holy because I am holy."

In Hebrew, there is a second word that is translated as holy, the word *qadosh*, which has more of a meaning of "sacred, pure, clean." Both the concept of being set apart for God as well as purity typify the lifestyle that we should exhibit. Those of us who have been called by God to serve Him cannot forget that He demands us to model a life of consecration before His people. It is no coincidence that He ordered Aaron to carry on his forehead the distinguishing mark of the leader who represents Jehovah: "You are to make a pure gold medallion and engrave it, like the engraving of a seal: HOLY TO THE LORD" (Exod. 28:36). Today, this mark or distinctive should be upon our minds and our hearts, reflected in our lifestyle. For the Christian, being set apart implies a distancing from sin and a drawing near to God, through a process that we call sanctification. This is the way that the New Testament presents the new birth. We need to abandon sin and begin to do works of righteousness, as Paul so clearly expresses in Ephesians: "Let the thief no longer steal. Instead, he is to do honest work with his own hands, so that he has something to share with anyone in need" (Eph. 4:28).

To those who stole when they were unbelievers, Paul not only commands them to stop stealing, but now that they are believers, he urges them to help those who are in need. Our sanctification is setting ourselves apart from the world so that we can draw near to God; we set ourselves apart from the world, we set ourselves apart from sin, and we draw near to the holiness of God. If this is true for the "ordinary person," it is even more true for the leader.

Holiness Has a Price

Walking in holiness has a price, but it does not even remotely resemble the price that Jesus paid for our salvation. A. W. Tozer said, "Loneliness seems to be one price the saint must pay for his saintliness."[2] When we decide to set ourselves apart for God, many people turn their backs on us; many people do not wish to follow us because they do not want to pay the price. God's leaders cannot compromise the Truth when they see that they are walking alone, as many have unfortunately done. Many prefer popularity and applause before loneliness in holiness. The contemporary church wants to feel more and more identified with the secular world, more accepted and more applauded. In summary, the local church wants to feel increasingly closer to the secular world. The sad reality is that the people of God do not tolerate being different; we still continue to say that we want to be like the other nations (1 Sam. 8:5, 20). As such, each time that the world does something new, the people of God desire a "Christian version" of the new secular music, of the new fashion, or whatever else.

God has left evidence in the lives of His people of the lengths to which He is willing to go in order to exalt His holiness and that it is never trivialized. Perhaps the best story illustrating this point appears in Leviticus 10:

> Aaron's sons Nadab and Abihu each took his own firepan, put fire in it, placed incense on it, and presented unauthorized fire before the LORD, which he had not commanded them to do. Then fire came from the LORD and consumed them, and they died before the LORD. Moses said to Aaron, "This is what the LORD has spoken:
>
>> I will demonstrate my holiness
>> to those who are near me,
>> and I will reveal my glory
>> before all the people."
>
> And Aaron remained silent. (vv. 1–3)

In this story, two sons of the high priest, also consecrated to the priesthood, appear and offer sacrifice to the true God in the true tabernacle with their respective censers that they have taken from the altar of incense. Nevertheless, God consumes them in the midst of a worship experience for having offered "unauthorized fire." Somehow, the sacrifice was not offered as God had prescribed, thus violating His holiness. We could speculate a little as we think about the censers and even wonder if it perhaps could have been the formula of incense that was not prescribed. God had said that the formula could only be used in the offering to Jehovah and that whoever used that same formula for other purposes would lose his life: "As for the incense you are making, you must not make any for yourselves using its formula. It is to be regarded by you as holy—belonging to the LORD. Anyone who makes something like it to smell its fragrance must be cut off from his people" (Exod. 30:37–38)

Today we do not offer incense, but the principle behind the incense offering remains: what we offer to God must be something special for Him. When we go to God, we are not just going to a neighbor. Rather, we are going to someone who deserves respect, reverence, honor, glory, and blessing. These principles find their application in the church today and in the many other things that we do for the Lord; therefore, we continually need to remember the warning of Leviticus 10:3. The leader of God's people should strive to present visible examples which show them that everything having to do with God should be handled with reverence, with "fear and trembling" (Phil. 2:12), to use a Pauline phrase.

Sometimes we ask ourselves: If we still lived in ancient times, how much of the worship offered to God today would result in a similar outcome? We do not know because it no longer happens that way. But it is possible because we believe that on many occasions what has been offered to God has simply been music and not a song of worship worthy of the God who is holy, holy, holy. In fact, one of our frequent complaints has been that, in many churches, the music is a bridge connecting one part of the service to the other and not necessarily a worship experience that prepares the believer's heart to receive the Word. We have even been in churches where the pastor does not participate in worship; he enters in the middle of it or afterward. This represents a trivialization of the worship that we offer to God.

In the text describing the death of Aaron's sons, the phrase "I will demonstrate my holiness to those who are near to me, and I will reveal my glory before all the people" is rather striking (Lev. 10:3). These are the words that Moses reiterates to Aaron when he apparently is about to complain because his two sons have died. Aaron was likely baffled because he had consecrated his two sons to the priesthood, and suddenly, they were no longer with him because Jehovah had "consumed" them in the midst of worship.

Moses hears a similar phrase on the day he strikes the rock twice (Num. 20) and speaks to the people in a way that is unacceptable to God. Jehovah had instructed him only to speak to the rock from which the water would flow, which is something the people needed at that moment. The irreverent manner in which Moses carried out this act cost him the Promised Land. Why? Because "I will demonstrate my holiness to those who are near me, and I will reveal my glory before all the people" (Lev. 10:3). These are words that Moses heard on the day that God informed him that he would not enter the Promised Land: "But the LORD said to Moses and Aaron, 'Because you did not trust me *to demonstrate my holiness in the sight of the Israelites,* you will not bring this assembly into the land I have given them'" (Num. 20:12, emphasis added). The testimony of God's leaders in the presence of the rest of the congregation is a matter of vital importance for God.

Perhaps we find ourselves wondering: Who taught Aaron's sons to treat the worship of God in such a trivial manner? Although we cannot answer such a question with the utmost certainty, we certainly can say that there was at least one incident in Aaron's life in which he greatly trivialized God's holiness. It happened early on during Israel's wandering through the wilderness when Aaron crafted a golden calf and an altar in the presence of the calf, telling the people, "There will be a festival to the LORD tomorrow" (Exod. 32:5). In just one day, Aaron reduced the image of God to a golden calf, something inconceivable to Him. The leaders of a God who describes Himself as three-times holy can never afford the luxury of treating His presence irreverently, especially in the presence of His people. Such speaks of how necessary it is for the leader to live in holiness so that he may know how to relate to God in a holy manner in the presence of His people. The former is necessary so that the people do not lose their fear of sin and so that they can maintain a reverent fear of their God. While it is true that the people of God have lost the fear of sin on multiple occasions throughout history, it is no less true that, with all certainty, the leaders of the people of God lost their reverence of our God well before.

Holiness Is the Number One Requirement for Communion with God

A life of holiness is the number one requirement for us to interact with God. Each person, place, or thing with which God interacts is called holy. Even a section of sand in the desert was described as such when Jehovah was present:

> When the LORD saw that he had gone over to
> look, God called out to him from the bush,
> "Moses, Moses!"
> "Here I am," he answered.
> "Do not come closer," he said. "Remove the
> sandals from your feet, for the place where you
> are standing is holy ground." (Exod. 3:4–5)

Moses could have very well passed through this place many times over the span of forty years, but on that particular day and that particular moment, it was declared holy because the presence of God was manifest there. In that instant, the place was associated with God, and everything that is closely related to Him is holy by definition. As such, in the New Testament, the apostle Paul's word of choice to refer to believers is *hagios*, which means "saints." We can therefore see that . . .

- His name is holy (Lev. 22:2).
- His Spirit is holy (Acts 2:33; 1 Cor. 6:19).
- His ways are holy (Ps. 77:13).
- His throne is holy (Ps. 47:8).
- His angels are holy (Deut. 33:2).

God dedicated an entire commandment to the protection of the holiness of His name because it represents what He is, just like His Word. Because of this, God has exalted both things (His name and His Word) above all else (Ps. 138:2). This should call us all to self-control, holiness, and seriousness much more than so often occurs. This call is even more true of leaders.

The list of persons and things that represent God and are called holy is endless. Following are a few examples:

1. His prophets are called holy (Acts 3:21).
2. The most holy place was found in the tabernacle (1 Chron. 6:49).
3. His people are called "a holy people belonging to the LORD" (Deut. 7:6).
4. The land where God led the Jewish people was called "the Holy Land" (Zech. 2:12).
5. God expects us to live a holy life (Rom. 12:1).

If this is so clear, why do the people of God and the leaders of the people not live in a holier way, especially in our day? Apparently to the extent that the church has become accustomed to living more like the world, the church has also become equally desensitized, as we will see later. This makes it easier for us to overlook the holiness of our great God.

The emphasis on this aspect of our great God is not found only in the Old Testament, as is the opinion of many, but also in the New Testament (Rom. 12:1; 1 Thess. 4:3; Heb. 12:28–29). In Romans 12:1, Paul commands us to offer our "bodies as a living sacrifice, holy and pleasing to God." Our mind, our heart, our will, and even the members of our body must be sanctified for use in service to our God. On the contrary, a lack of sanctification becomes a stumbling block. Charles Spurgeon said, "Beware of no man more than of yourself; we carry our worst enemies within us."[3] Today, many live their lives irresponsibly attributing their failures to Satan, when in reality, we are the ones truly responsible for cultivating a life of holiness under the leading and power of the Holy Spirit. Of course, Satan is capable of tempting us, but we can either yield to or resist his temptations. It was Satan who tempted Adam and Eve and made them fall. But in the end, God called out and imposed consequences upon this first couple who were unable to resist temptation, as they believed Satan more than they believed God.

Holiness Requires Discipline

Holiness must be cultivated and requires both limits and discipline. As such, it is a continuous effort in which we should always be aware of the things to which we expose ourselves: conversations, people, images, movies, written materials, etc. Repetitive exposure to sin, in whatever form, desensitizes us over time, and we grow accustomed to greater levels of sin. It is interesting to note the history of ladies' swimsuits. Years ago, these swimsuits covered the entire body, including the wrists and ankles. Little by little, they have been shortened to the point that they are now just small pieces of fabric. But today, not even nudity at the beach causes many to blush. The desensitization has become so great that even Christian parents take their children to these beaches with no sense of modesty, using the excuse that there is nowhere else to go. The child who is exposed to this type of sensuality at the age of six will want to experience many other things at twelve years of age, and even more at sixteen.

This is why the Bible tells us that "[b]ad company corrupts good morals" (1 Cor. 15:33), recognizing how greatly the flesh is influenced toward sin and wickedness.

Paul, as Timothy's teacher, instructed him regarding the need to live a disciplined life when he tells him in 1 Timothy 4:7: "train yourself in godliness." In one of his books, Kent Hughes makes a very interesting comment when he explains that the phrase "train yourself" comes from the Greek word *gumnos*, which means "naked." In ancient times, Greek athletes trained practically naked in order to avoid any possible obstacle. Perhaps Paul had the idea in mind that we get rid of anything that would be of any hindrance to us, just as the author of Hebrews maintains: "Therefore, since we also have such a large cloud of witnesses surrounding us, let us lay aside every hindrance and the sin that so easily ensnares us. Let us run with endurance the race that lies before us" (Heb. 12:1).

The author appears to separate those things which are sinful from those things that, although not sinful in and of themselves, represent a great hindrance to our life of sanctification. Watching a football game is not a sin, but some men are such big sports fans that they neglect spending the time that they should spend with God and their family in order to sit in front of the television. Sports are not sinful, but they frequently have been a hindrance to our walk with God. When such is the case, we need to get rid of that which is robbing precious time from our lives. Note how the author of Hebrews separates that which is just a hindrance from that which is sin. In other words, there are things in our lives that are hindrances and perhaps not sin but do represent an obstacle, an inconvenience, or a barrier to our sanctification. Another example could be television, which is not sinful in and of itself, but it can become an enormous sin, not necessarily because of the programs that we watch, but for the hours we spend in front of it which cause us to become ever more irresponsible in many different areas of our life. A. W. Tozer said, "The abuse of a harmless thing is sin."[4]

The Word of God commands us to exercise godliness and holiness such that there is nothing in our path that would represent an obstacle which would reduce the speed of our advance, or a hindrance that would cause us to stumble. Nothing of quality is ever produced without the necessary effort. If our lives of holiness are to have any quality (not merits), we will have the obligation to invest time in reflection, study, and meditation in order to arrive at such a place. Nevertheless, the disciplined Christian life is the exception and not the rule, even more so when we are talking about males, a reality we can confirm in counseling. There is no discipline in prayer life, the study of the Word, and the management of financial resources.

Discipline has to do with our love for God and not with our desire to impress others. This is the difference between discipline and legalism. Discipline places God at the center, whereas legalism places man at the center. When we speak of discipline, we are not referring to punishing the body as Martin Luther did before coming to know Christ; rather, we are speaking of an organized life that has its priorities in order, God at the center, without excess, with self-control so that the desires of the flesh do not cause us to fall, and with a balance between grace and truth.

What Can We Do to Avoid Stumbling?

Beloved, we need to wake up and seek out people with whom we can converse, vent, be accountable, and mutually encourage one another. A more experienced pastor can be a great mentor. It has been said that each one of us should have three close friends: a Paul to mentor us, a Barnabas to encourage us, and a Timothy whom we can train. Regrettably, the majority of men do not have a close friend because they are fearful of revealing their weaknesses and struggles. This often causes us to be isolated from others, which makes us vulnerable on our own little island. We think that we are self-sufficient; we do things without praying, without reflection, without consulting others because we tend to be individualists. Women have very good friends and, in general, they know their inner lives. Although men say that they have good friends, they do not know anything about the inner lives of their "good friends." Men usually do not communicate, discuss, or reveal what is going on in their lives, and their intimate friendships are limited to spending time with others doing the things which they have in common, such as a hobby, work, or something similar. We have all heard of that person who does not have any close friends because he fears that if everyone knew how he truly is, they probably would not want to be friends with him. Can you imagine what it must be like to live in that kind of prison? Isolation makes us more vulnerable to falling.

Christ knew our vulnerability, which is why He taught: "And if your eye causes you to fall away, gouge it out" (Mark 9:47a). We cannot negotiate with sin; nor can we trivialize it or, much less, ignore it. One sin for one night can cause us to lose our ministry and our family. Do not risk it. That eye could represent several things. For many, it is television or the computer. For others, it is a secretary or an assistant; while for others, it is the gym or finances. The list is endless. We cannot flirt with sin. The Word says: "Can a man embrace fire and his clothes not be burned?" (Prov. 6:27).

We have to establish limits to our communication. If you are married, do not share your innermost thoughts with someone of the opposite sex. If you are single, be careful how you spend your leisure time, where you hang out, and how you spend your time with people of the opposite sex. Married people also should not form intimate friendships with people of the opposite sex. When you travel, beware of your involvement with the opposite sex, especially in our day when many women are aggressive and, in many cases, have been so forward as to be the ones to invite men to engage in forbidden activities. Today, we must have more limits than in days past.

Final Reflection

The effectiveness of our life is directly proportional to its holiness. God takes no pleasure in unholiness, and if He is not so honored, He will not cause His grace and power to flow through us. We must keep our lives holy if we want to be used by God.

Warren Wiersbe mentions that ministry takes place "when divine resources meet human needs through loving channels to the glory of God";[5] and this will not occur if there is not holiness within leadership. Much of the stagnation in today's church is due precisely to the lack of holiness in the pulpit and pew. Leaders who are not holy hinder the work of God.

The Holy Spirit is our agent of sanctification, and if He does not operate, nothing will occur because, apart from Christ, we can do nothing (John 15:5). But at the same time, the believer has a role to play in sanctification, which requires sacrifice, surrender, accountability, submission, and discipline. As we have said before, this does not happen by osmosis. We should set ourselves apart from the world and its sinful ways and attach ourselves to the true Vine so that we can bear much fruit.

CHAPTER 5

Be a Servant of His Presence

"Now if I have indeed found favor with you, please teach
me your ways, and I will know you, so that I may find
favor with you. Now consider that this nation is your
people." And he replied, "My presence will go with you,
and I will give you rest." "If your presence does not go,"
Moses responded to him, "don't make us go up from here."

Exodus 33:13–15

Introduction

When we speak of "a servant of His presence" we are referring to the believer who longs to live in the presence of God and
is willing to pay whatever price necessary to stay there. Given
His omnipresence, God is always present in every inch of the
universe, but when we speak of the manifest presence of God, we
are referring to His activity made known in new conversions, the
repentance of sinful habits on the part of believers, the strength-
ening of marriages, the joy in the life of the church, and growth

in the image of Christ in an evident way. These things are not necessarily present in each believer, nor are they present in each church. It is difficult to define how the believer's longing for the presence of God manifests itself, but Moses is a good example of a believer who possessed this characteristic.

The more we study the life of Moses, the more we are impressed by his life, his testimony as a leader, his wisdom, and his legacy. The intimacy with God that Moses displayed impresses us, as well as his requests, his resolutions, his patience, his passion for God's people, and his incessant desire to know God better and to live in intimacy with Him.

Some will remember that there was an extraordinarily sinful event in the life of the Hebrew people early on during the forty years of wandering in the wilderness. Moses had gone up on the mountain to speak to God, and as the days wore on, the people became impatient with Aaron, the high priest and brother of Moses. This man, who had been chosen by God, not only gave in to the pressure, but also made it clear that although he had left Egypt, Egypt had not left him. All the idolatry that the people had learned in more than four hundred years of slavery in a foreign land came to light on that day when Aaron crafted a calf from all of the gold that the people offered for such an occasion (Exod. 32).

As a consequence, God threatened the people that He would not continue on with them to the Promised Land in order to avoid destroying them along the way because, as they were such a sinful people, their actions constantly provoked God. This news caused great sadness among the people. Therefore, Moses set out to speak with God in response to the proclamation that God had just made to them.

In the text of Exodus 33:12–23, the requests that Moses makes to God certainly capture our attention:

- "[I]f I have indeed found favor with you" (v. 13).
- "[T]each me your ways" (v. 13).

- "If your presence does not go, don't make us go up from here" (v. 15).
- "Please, let me see your glory" (v. 18).

There is not one self-centered request made by Moses. Each and every one of them had to do with the person of God, which speaks of a servant who lives in a God-centered way and allows us to see that he is a man "of the presence of God."

In this book, which deals with "being before doing," it is important to emphasize the need for all of us who desire to serve the Lord to have our service flow from our daily and ongoing relationship with our God. It is incredible that every time we learn of the Fall of a servant of God, we invariably learn that his prayer life had waned, and he was no longer walking in intimacy with the Lord. When we walk with God, His presence drives sin from us; when we practice sin, it separates us from God. Such was true in the Old Testament. It remained true in the New Testament, and it has continued to be the case throughout church history. That being said, walking with God is not having daily devotions, although it can be a part of a life of intimacy with Him. Many people who have daily devotions don't exhibit the character of Christ in their lives because often during their quiet time, they read the Bible and mark it in all sorts of colors, but unfortunately, that same Bible does not mark the life of the one who reads it, leading to frequent falls and failures. There is nothing worse than developing a pharisaic lifestyle because following a daily prayer and devotional routine often convinces us that we are doing well, when, in reality, such activities have become rituals instead of being spiritual exercises which please God.

How a Servant of His Presence Thinks

In order to address this particular point, we are going to look at a somewhat lengthy passage found in Exodus 33 so that we can continue to refer back to it throughout this chapter. After the

incident with the golden calf (Exod. 32), God decided to distance
Himself from the people of Israel, and He informs Moses of His
decision (Exod. 33). Before the announcement, Moses reacted,
and the words that follow reflect the dialogue between the two
of them:

> Moses said to the LORD, "Look, you have told
> me, 'Lead this people up,' but you have not let
> me know whom you will send with me. You said,
> 'I know you by name, and you have also found
> favor with me.' Now if I have indeed found favor
> with you, please teach me your ways, and I will
> know you, so that I may find favor with you. Now
> consider that this nation is your people."
>
> And he replied, "My presence will go with
> you, and I will give you rest."
>
> "If your presence does not go," Moses
> responded to him, "don't make us go up from
> here. How will it be known that I and your
> people have found favor with you unless you go
> with us? I and your people will be distinguished
> by this from all the other people on the face of
> the earth."
>
> The LORD answered Moses, "I will do this
> very thing you have asked, for you have found
> favor with me, and I know you by name."
>
> Then Moses said, "Please, let me see your
> glory."
>
> He said, "I will cause all my goodness to pass
> in front of you, and I will proclaim the name 'the
> LORD' before you. I will be gracious to whom I
> will be gracious, and I will have compassion on
> whom I will have compassion." But he added,
> "You cannot see my face, for humans cannot see
> me and live." The LORD said, "Here is a place
> near me. You are to stand on the rock, and when

my glory passes by, I will put you in the crevice
of the rock and cover you with my hand until I
have passed by. Then I will take my hand away,
and you will see my back, but my face will not
be seen." (Exod. 33:12–23)

God told Moses that He would not go in their midst and
that, in His place, He would send an angel to accompany them
until they reached the Promised Land. Thus, God kept His
promise of getting them there but changed the relationship from
intimacy to estrangement. An angel would now go with them
instead of His manifest presence. God considered the Israelites
His people, but now He was so disgusted with them that He no
longer called them "my people," and simply started to refer to
them as "the people you brought up from the land of Egypt," as
Exodus 33:1 indicates. This reflects the fact that God had begun
to separate Himself from the people and manifests this in the following words: "I will send an angel ahead of you and will drive
out the Canaanites, Amorites, Hethites, Perizzites, Hivites, and
Jebusites. Go up to a land flowing with milk and honey. But I will
not go up with you because you are a stiff-necked people; otherwise, I might destroy you on the way" (Exod. 33:2–3). Moses
understood the message perfectly, and as he understood it, he
became concerned, troubled, and saddened. With all of these
emotions swelling on the inside, Moses responded to the Lord,
"Look, you have told me, 'Lead this people up,' but you have not
let me know whom you will send with me" (Exod. 33:12a). Moses
was worried because, although God told him that He would send
an angel who would go before them into the Promised Land, He
did not reveal the identity of the angel. So, Moses showed Him
that there was something that was of great concern, that God was
not with them.

One might think that Moses was somewhat presumptuous
in asking the Lord such questions and that he should have been
content with the fact that God Himself promised to send them
an angel, but this did not satisfy him because he had never

before followed an angel. He wanted God's presence, and nothing other than His presence would satisfy him. An angel was a symbol of divine protection to the extent that, when God promises the angel, He states that through the angel He will cast out all of the tribes that were occupying the Promised Land at that time. Therefore, the angel represented a blessing or protection. Nevertheless, Moses was not looking for a blessing; he wanted to be the one doing the blessing. While blessings are good, the pursuit after the one who blesses is better. Moses did not desire what was good; he desired the best.

> Before God could answer, the prophet went on to make it clear that he would not settle for anything less than the very presence of God. He didn't want any old angel to help him; he wanted the direct guidance of Almighty God [. . .]. To lead the people effectively, Moses needed to know the very mind of God. He didn't want God simply to send down orders; he wanted to know the thinking behind God's plans—his ways with his people. To that end, Moses wanted to remain in constant communication with God. This was essential to his spiritual leadership.[1]

Many leaders and other believers desire time with God, but during such time of intimacy, they typically seek more after His blessings than after God Himself. Perhaps this is the reason why we tend to seek after God more frequently when we are in need than when things are going well. It is as if we are saying to God that we do not need Him as much when things are going well. So, on occasion, God has to allow certain difficulties in our lives in order to again produce in us the desire to be with Him. If this is how we normally seek after God, we should realize that we are not truly seeking after Him but after His blessings. This kind of disciple would have been perfectly fine with the angel's company, but Moses was not. It is a serious problem that the children of God settle for so little in their relationship with Him. If God solved all of his children's problems without having an intimate relationship with them, the majority of them would settle for simply having their problems solved without experiencing His manifest presence. How sad and unfortunate that would be! In the garden of Eden, Adam and Eve had all of their problems solved, and they also had the presence of God with them. In the eternal kingdom, we will have all of our problems solved, and we will still need the presence of God.

The greatest evidence that Moses did not seek anything other than the presence of the Almighty God is found in the following words:

> "You said, 'I know you by name, and you have also found favor with me.' Now if I have indeed found favor with you, please teach me your ways, and I will know you, so that I may find favor with you." (Exod. 33:12b–13a)

Moses could have told the Lord, "If it is true that I have found favor with You, do not make me have to deal with so much work in this desert." But he did not. He could have asked God to make him arrive early to the Promised Land, but he did not do that, either. Or, he perhaps could have required the Lord to show him how much further he had to go to reach the Promised Land, but we do not hear of that in the account. All of these requests are insignificant. Moses desired only one thing: the presence of God.

Remember, Moses spoke to God face-to-face just as a person would speak to his or her friend; in the text that we are observing, we see that this truly was the case. Moses says to God: "You said, 'I know you by name, and you have also found favor with me'" (Exod. 33:12b). We do not know exactly when God spoke these words, but He apparently did at some point, perhaps in the Tent of Meeting. The phrase "I know you by name" is an expression that demonstrates that God intimately knew Moses and loved him in a special way, to the extent that He had looked upon Moses with grace. Moses repeats the words of God and thus says to Him, "[I]f I have indeed found favor with you, please teach me your ways, and I will know you, so that I may find favor with you" (Exod. 33:13). What an extraordinary request! Moses desired to know God's ways, how He operates, how He works, how He orchestrates history.

Be a Servant Who Desires to Know God's Ways

A servant of His presence knows his own weakness and need for God.

Moses not only asks God to show him His ways, but he pleads with God that He would make known His ways to him. God must make us to know His ways because, otherwise, we would never come to know them. This means that . . .

- God must reveal His ways to us, or we will never be able to see them for ourselves.
- God must orchestrate circumstances in our lives that obligate us to go in His direction, or we will always take the wrong way.

Moses knew that the Lord's ways are not our ways (Isa. 55:8); and, therefore, he was interested in knowing them so that he could serve the Lord better. Knowing God's ways is essential to obedience. It is striking how rarely the great men of God asked for the material things that we ask for daily. Jesus assured us that the material things we pray for would be added unto us. The kingdom of God and His righteousness (Matt. 6:33) should be at the center of our search.

Now, Moses wanted to know these ways because he had a deep desire to know God more. This is why he says: "[P]lease teach me your ways, and I will know you" (Exod. 33:13b). Knowing God intimately assures us greater communion with Him, and it is in intimate communion with God where passion for Him is forged. Little passion is the result of little communion.

A servant of His presence possesses a continuous thirst for God.

This last request of Moses is extraordinary ("please teach me your ways, and I will know you"), seeing that he had spoken with God in the desert at the burning bush, that God had spoken with him prior to the ten plagues that fell upon Egypt, that Moses had spent forty days with God on the top of Mount Sanai, and that he had spoken face-to-face with God. Even so, Moses asks God to teach him His ways so that he would better know Him. Moses' desire to know God was insatiable. So, we can understand why God found favor with Moses and why Moses found grace in God's eyes. We know that God's grace is always undeserved, but there is an aspect for which man is responsible in the exercise of his will, and that aspect may please or displease God. The best illustration of this are the sacrifices of Cain and Abel. Genesis 4:4b–5a says: "The LORD had regard for Abel and his offering. . . . Cain was furious, and he looked despondent." This clearly implies that there are ways of walking with God which cause His favor to fall upon us, and there are others which cause His discipline to fall upon us. Moses' requests did not seek the solution to his problems, but that God would allow Moses to know Him more.

If we had a deep desire to know Him, perhaps we would have fewer problems in our daily life because God would open up our ways. Take note of the Lord's words from the mouth of the prophet Jeremiah:

"'This is what the LORD says:
The wise person should not boast in his
       wisdom;
the strong should not boast in his strength;
the wealthy should not boast in his wealth.
But the one who boasts should boast in this:
that he understands and knows me—
that I am the LORD, showing faithful love,
justice, and righteousness on the earth,

for I delight in these things.
This is the LORD's declaration.'" (Jer. 9:23–24)

God's number one desire for His children is that we would come to know Him even more. This is the best way to guarantee that Christ's character is formed in us. It is also the best way to live in the fullness that Christ purchased for those whom He redeemed (John 10:10). God has given us His written Word, which represents the best revelation of His character. If we are missing the desire to read His Word, we should ask God to give it to us because, as the book of James so well indicates, we have not because we ask not (James 4:2).

Let us think for a moment about the last time we asked God to show us more of Himself, that He would open our eyes. When? For each of these requests, how many hundreds of other requests have we made to Him? We need to learn to view prayer as an exercise for experiencing spiritual growth and intimacy with God more than an exercise to get what we want. Sadly, our search is frequently too centered on asking God to solve our problems.

In order to know if God was pleased with Moses' prayer, we need only to pay attention to the words that form part of His response to Moses: "My presence will go with you, and I will give you rest" (Exod. 33:14b). After having told the people that He would send an angel ahead of them and that He would not go with them, once again, God promises that He will send His presence with them in response to Moses' prayer. In this way, God partially shows the nature of His ways.

A servant of His presence desires to know the will of God so that he may obey it.

When Moses asked God to show him His ways, in essence, he was asking God to show him His will. This should be every Christian's request at all times: "Lord, I want to know Your will." Let us remember that, when the disciples came to Christ and asked Him to teach them to pray, part of His response was: "[P]ray like this: Our Father in heaven, your name be honored as holy. Your kingdom come. Your will be done on earth as it is in heaven. Give us today our daily bread" (Matt. 6:9–11). Christ taught His disciples that, before making requests for their personal needs, they should focus on seeking out the will of God. On occasion, the difficult situations in which we find ourselves are part of God's will of forming the character of Christ in us. Nevertheless, we frequently ask Him to remove us from the difficult situation without even asking ourselves if the difficulty could, in fact, be a part of His will. Similarly, we sometimes ask for sanctification, and we forget that part of the answer may represent difficulties that not only respond to our request for sanctification but form part of purposes of which we are unaware, as was the case with Job. Our faith, which is more precious than gold, is forged in the middle of the fires of trial, just as Peter says to his followers (1 Pet. 1:7).

A servant of His presence enjoys the blessings of doing the will of God.

The result of walking in God's ways is rest: "My presence will go with you, and I will give you rest" (Exod. 33:14b). Our emotional or spiritual weariness is not necessarily the product of spiritual struggles, as is often taught today, although there certainly are spiritual struggles. Rather, it is the result of several possibilities all at the same time: not walking in His ways, doing things in the flesh and not in the Spirit, doing more than what God has ordered us to do, or not walking in His presence.

Moses knew the price of not walking in the presence of God, and it was a price he was not willing to pay: "'If your presence does not go,' Moses responded to him, 'don't make us go up from here'" (Exod. 33:15). This servant of God knew perfectly well the principle embodied in Psalm 127: "Unless the LORD builds a house, its builders labor over it in vain" (v. 1).

*A servant of His presence is interested in the fame of His name
and not his own.*

Closely observe the following rationale of Moses: "How will
it be known that I and your people have found favor with you
unless you go with us? I and your people will be distinguished
by this from all the other people on the face of the earth" (Exod.
33:16). Moses grows through each trial. His concern is for it to be
clearly established that Jehovah is not like all of the other gods
and that the people of God are not like all of the other peoples.
He knew that the way other peoples would recognize that God
was with the Israelites was not by preventing them from lacking
bread, water, or other everyday staples. He recognized that the
difference between them and the other peoples was that the presence of God may or may not go with them. This is why he says:
"Is it not in your going with us, so that we are distinct, I and your
people, from every other people on the face of the earth?" (Exod.
33:16b ESV). If the presence of the Lord was not with them, their
lives certainly would look like the lives of all of the other peoples.
Therefore, this is why the lives of certain Christians look similar
to the lives of unbelievers, because the presence of God is not
with them in an ostensible way. His salvation may be with them,
but not His manifest presence.

A servant of the presence of God desires the glory of God and not his own.

Thanks to Moses' intercession before God on behalf of the
people, He once again affirms that His presence will accompany
them up to the Promised Land. However, it appears that Moses
had his doubts about this, as only a few moments earlier God
had told him that He would no longer go with them. Perhaps this
is the reason why he makes the following request: "Moses said,
'Please show me your glory'" (Exod. 33:18 ESV). Moses first asks
God to show him His ways so that he could know him better
(v. 13b), and he ultimately implores the Lord to show him His
glory so that he could better worship Him.

He said, "I will cause all my goodness to pass in front of you, and I will proclaim the name 'the Lord' before you. I will be gracious to whom I will be gracious, and I will have compassion on whom I will have compassion." (Exod. 33:19)

When Moses descended from Mount Sinai after conversing with the Lord there for forty days and forty nights, his face shone so brightly that the people could not look at him and he had to cover himself with a veil (Exod. 34:29–35). Living in the presence of God transforms those who experience it. In fact, the apostle Paul teaches in one of his letters that we are transformed beholding the face of God, and the way to do so today is to spend time immersed in His Word. These are the words of Paul to the Corinthians: "And we all, with unveiled face, beholding the glory of the Lord, are being transformed into the same image from one degree of glory to another. For this comes from the Lord who is the Spirit" (2 Cor. 3:18).

God began showing His ways to Moses from the very moment He called out to him from the midst of the burning bush (Exod. 3:1–12). Knowing God's ways is vitally important for those of us who desire to walk with God in intimacy of heart. Therefore, let us look at some of the ways of God:

The Ways of God

1. God's ways are holy.

The first words that Moses heard from God were the following: "Moses, Moses!" "Here I am," he answered. "Do not come closer," he said. "Remove the sandals from your feet, for the place where you are standing is holy ground" (Exod. 3:4b–5). If we want to discern the will of God, we have to walk in holiness. This principle is nonnegotiable. The difficulty we have discovering His will is often due to the fact that the path we are traveling is not holy. In order to illustrate this, we could say that God

over

refuses to broadcast his voice on a "frequency of carnality." We all know that radios have frequencies, AM and FM, and it is as if the world has two radio frequencies: CF or carnal frequency, where Satan "broadcasts" his will, and HF or holy frequency, where God "broadcasts" His. To which of these two frequencies do you "tune" your mind and heart? This is a simple illustration, but it serves us in emphasizing the point.

Henry Blackaby, in his book *The Ways of God*, says that "Holiness is God's requirement for relationship." Blackaby adds: "Because of sin, our ways can even seem right in our own eyes, but the result of our ways will be destruction."[2] The first time that God threatened the people with separation from Him was precisely due to a lack of holiness (Exod. 33:3). Israel had not assessed the enormous privilege of having the great I AM in their midst. "The principle here is that the greater our spiritual privilege, the greater the adverse consequences when we fail."[3]

The prophet Isaiah said it this way: "But your iniquities are separating you from your God, and your sins have hidden his face from you so that he does not listen" (Isa. 59:2). Holiness in the life of the believer is the evidence of the manifest presence of God because it is He who makes us holy. A holy people reflects the essence of the character of God, and it is precisely to this that we were called: "But you are a chosen race, a royal priesthood, a holy nation, a people for his possession, so that you may proclaim the praises of the one who called you out of darkness into his marvelous light" (1 Pet. 2:9). There exist two forms of announcing His virtues: proclaiming them and reflecting them. When our lives reflect little holiness, they demonstrate that we do not know His ways or that we are not walking in them.

2. God's ways are sovereign.

When Moses was called, at first, he refused to go. At that moment, God began to show him that His ways are sovereign: "But Moses replied to the LORD, 'Please, Lord, I have never been eloquent—either in the past or recently or since you have been speaking to your servant—because my mouth and my tongue are sluggish.' The LORD said to him, "Who placed a mouth on humans? Who makes a person mute or deaf, seeing or blind? Is it not I, the LORD?'" (Exod. 4:10–11). With this, Moses should have begun to understand that, if he desired to walk with God, he would have to stop questioning Him. As Augustine said, "We count on God's mercy for our past mistakes, on God's love for our present needs, on God's sovereignty for our future."[4] We may ask God questions when we do not understand, but we do not have the right to question Him. With each of the plagues that He brought upon Egypt, God confirmed to Moses that His ways were sovereign and showed His sovereignty over all creation. When we act out of rebelliousness, we demonstrate that we do not know His ways.

God decides if He will accompany us along the way or if He will not. What determines whether or not God will go with us is our level of obedience to His will. The disobedience of the Hebrew people caused them to make it to the Promised Land forty years and 600,000 deaths later. The people's disobedience ended up exhausting Moses, who also disobeyed what the Lord had commanded him to do, and that cost him the Promised Land because God's ways are ways of obedience. God does not negotiate our obedience. He neither gives us options nor does He present His commands as multiple-choice tests, but as single-answer tests.

3. God's ways are faithful.

Even in the worst of circumstances, God reminded the people that He would send an angel before them to carry them to the land promised to Abraham, Isaac, and Jacob. God kept His word; He finishes what He starts. The question: Will we keep our word with God and others? The Lord decided to accompany the people again after listening to Moses' request precisely because He is faithful to His promises. When we are unfaithful,

He remains faithful (2 Tim. 2:13). Our unfaithfulness is evidence that we do not know His ways, and we do not know Him.

4. God's ways are inscrutable.

In fact, this is exactly what Romans 11:33b (ESV) says: "How unsearchable are his judgments and how inscrutable his ways!" His wisdom surpasses ours. It is He who writes history, and when He writes it, He knows the end even at the beginning. God led the children of Israel into the desert, and guided them to the shores of the Red Sea, with mountains at their front and the Egyptians at their back. Exodus 13:18 tells us that it was God who made them go in that direction. This decision appears completely illogical to human reasoning, but God made it because He knew that He would open up the Red Sea so that the children of Israel could cross and that He would later close it on top of the Egyptians when they were in close pursuit. No one could have predicted such a movement of God. This one act demonstrated His power, His wisdom, His faithfulness to His people, and His justice to those who hate Him. Sometimes dead-end streets are evidence of God's leading us in showing us that He is the God who can work even when there is no hope. When we want God to give us an explanation about everything that is to occur, we demonstrate that we really do not know His ways. It is incredible to see how, after walking with God for forty years, the people still did not know Him or His ways. This is why the passing of time does not guarantee the knowledge of God. Instead, it is the intimacy that we have developed with Him. *Amen*

Final Reflection

God's ways are a representation of His will, and this is a reflection of His character. We cannot completely know His ways, but we can trust Him because He has revealed His character in His Word and specifically in the history that He has built between Himself and His people, something that is available to us.

A servant who does not trust in the character of God is not ready to serve. God first had to convince Moses that He truly is the great I AM (Exod. 3:14), perhaps working miracles by His power and perhaps grieving deeply for the oppression of the Hebrew people at the hand of the Egyptians. Once Moses was convinced of this, he was willing to return to the children of Israel and stand before Pharaoh with just his staff in his hand. It is interesting to see how the staff that Moses had used for many years (Exod. 4:2, 17), and that we could call "the staff of Moses," soon became known as "the staff of God" (Exod. 4:20). From that moment on, it would be the staff of God because He would use it as a symbol of performing His miracles or the symbol of His faithfulness as shepherd of the people.

If God is the author of our story and we do not know the entire story, it is logical to think that our major pursuit should be seeking after His presence. On the other hand, there is no one in the universe who has the stature of our God. He is the author of all that exists outside of Himself. Also, in no other place do we find what we find in Him: forgiveness, redemption, eternal life, peace, joy, significance, meaning, purpose, etc. . . . this list could be endless. "'[I]n Him we live and move and have our being'" (Acts 17:28a). Once again, following His ways is to follow His will, and His will is good, acceptable, and perfect (Rom. 12:2 ESV). At the end of our days, "we will look back and conclude that our lives were well lived and be satisfied with them."[5] A life well-lived is the topic of the next chapter.

CHAPTER 6

Be a Servant of a Life Well-Lived

"[E]veryone who bears my name and is created for my glory.
I have formed them; indeed, I have made them."
Isaiah 43:7

Introduction

The texts of Isaiah let us see that a life well-lived, in essence, is a life lived for the glory of the Creator. The reason is a simple one: God formed us and later called us to the praise of His glory. If we live any other way, we are outside of the purpose for which we were created, and a life like that cannot produce satisfaction. When God thought of us in eternity past, He immediately thought of a purpose for which we should live. Therefore, if we are alive in this generation, it is because God understands that He needs us, not in the same way that we need Him, but in the sense that God made us to be born at this time and not at another in order to fulfill a purpose through us in His history. The unsatisfaction that people possess is multifaceted, but an important reason is that many live outside of God's purposes. On one occasion, Jesus Himself revealed that His coming into the world had only one purpose: to do the will of the Father. These were His exact words: "My food is to do the will of him who sent me and to finish his work" (John 4:34). If this was the case for Jesus, it should be for us, also. Not living this way will bring us dissatisfaction and consequences.

A few years ago, the book *Your Best Life Now* was published. The focus of this and many other books of our day is highly man-centered, emphasizing what we want and the potential that we supposedly possess to gain success and prosperity according to our own definition of it. We all have an idea of how or where we would like to live; but if that is not God's plan for us, we ultimately will have not lived well. As such, a life well-lived has to be aligned with God's will, and, therefore, it must be consistent with the plans that He has for us. Moreover, a life well-lived cannot be centered on our inner person, neither can it have a horizontal focus over a vertical one. The only possibility of living well is to have a vertical focus which then allows us to relate correctly in our horizontal focus. This is why a life well-lived is one that is lived for God's glory, and this concept is much more solemn than we think. To live for the glory of God is to swim against the current of the rest of humanity; we are swimming upstream.

Now, it is very important for us to arrive at an understanding that living for the glory of God is the only way to experience the fullness of life that Christ speaks of in John 10:10. This way of living naturally produces spiritual joy. We tag things as "spiritual" to make it clear that when we speak of joy, we are not thinking of fanfare and celebration, although there is certainly a time for such things. When we speak of joy, we are referring to an internal satisfaction with the life that God has given us. Therefore, if we live for the glory of God, we should naturally see fruit and results in our life, things that we need not even seek after, but things that are the natural result of a life well-lived. One of these is that we experience an almost continuous spiritual satisfaction with the life God has granted us, bringing us emotional and spiritual stability. In other words, the life of a child of God which is characterized by continuous highs and lows cannot be a life well-lived. The verse of Scripture that best defines what living well looks like is found in Paul's first letter to the Corinthians: "So, whether you eat or drink, or whatever you do, do everything for the glory of God" (1 Cor. 10:31). Here, the apostle Paul defines how to do the simplest tasks of everyday life. This applies both to the mother raising her children and the businessman, who both should carry out their plans having the glory of God as their number one goal. "What is not, or cannot be, for the glory of the one and only God probably should be excluded from "whatever you do."[1]

Be Cautious with Your Goals

Running the Christian race with a goal in mind is a biblical concept. Paul expressed it in the following way:

> Don't you know that the runners in a stadium all race, but only one receives the prize? Run in such a way to win the prize. Now everyone who competes exercises self-control in everything. They do it to receive a perishable crown, but we an imperishable crown. So I do not run like one who runs aimlessly or box like one beating the air. Instead, I discipline my body and bring it under strict control, so that after preaching to others, I myself will not be disqualified. (1 Cor. 9:24–27)

"So run that you may obtain it," says Paul. His words reflect a sense of urgency. However, many Christians do not live with this sense of urgency, and this does not go along with a life well-lived. The present counts forever. Therefore, we should not be spiritually idle. The text above says that "everyone who competes exercises self-control in everything" (v. 25a), that is, as the athlete trains, he does not exercise only his body but also self-control in order to accomplish the goal. "The same need for self- control is no less relevant in the modern world where immediate hedonistic gratification is a given and fulfilling one's desires is taken to be a healthy response irrespective of the context or social implications."[2]

An Olympic athlete is willing to sacrifice hours of sleep to be at practice; he also abstains from certain foods in order to avoid gaining weight while even giving up certain types of entertainment. He does everything necessary without complaining because he enjoys it. The apostle Paul seems to insinuate, then, that we as Christians should be willing to abstain from whatever is necessary for the cause of Christ. This is a good goal. If athletes run "to receive a perishable crown, but we an imperishable crown" (v. 25b), should we not be willing to make a greater sacrifice if it is necessary? This is why Paul and the rest of the martyrs ultimately gave their lives, because they understood that the crown that they were to receive in glory was greater than the temporary crown won by Olympic runners. Paul continues by saying: "I do not run like one who runs aimlessly" (v. 26a). Here, we clearly see that the apostle had a defined life goal, one which he would passionately pursue. Paul was willing to submit his body to discipline, aided by the grace of God, so that he would not give in to the desires of the flesh and end up disqualified.

Moreover, we need to understand that Paul was not talking about willpower, but of self-control, which is a fruit of the Spirit. In all of this, there is a sense of self-control. But if we do not have this sense of self-control in our life, it is possible that we will not finish the race well. In the New Testament, we are called to be self-controlled nine times (1 Cor. 9:25; 1 Thess. 5:6, 8; 1 Tim. 3:2; 2 Tim. 4:5; Titus 2:2; 1 Pet. 1:13 (NLT); 4:7 (ESV); and 5:8). Paul even says to young Timothy, "But as for you, exercise self-control in everything, endure hardship, do the work of an evangelist, fulfill your ministry" (2 Tim. 4:5). We cannot run the race well if we are not self-controlled and pursue God's purposes as our goal.

The urgent goal of today's large companies is to reach their specified goals each year. But God does not operate like man. For God, goals are as important as the process we go through to reach them. Therefore, our goals need to have a biblical frame of reference. Sadly, some Christian leaders lay out goals for their lives or ministries which, perhaps, come from God, only later to pursue them in a sinful way, and, as a result, they get only half-way toward the goal because they stumble and fall. God finishes what He starts. He has never started something without finishing it. As such, on a personal level, we have come to the conclusion that every human effort that falls along the wayside does so because God did not initiate it. If God has to remove Moses in order to continue on toward the Promised Land with Joshua, He will do it, as He did, in effect, according to the Old Testament.

God does not start something that He does not intend on finishing. We stop projects right in the middle because we get discouraged, become fatigued, are surprised by things that we did not anticipate, or we run out of resources. But those things that habitually happen to human beings do not happen to God. He clearly says: "I am God, and there is no other; I am God, and no one is like me. I declare the end from the beginning, and from long ago what is not yet done, saying: my plan will take place, and I will do all my will" (Isa. 46:9b–10). Thus, God has never conceived a purpose in His mind that has not been carried out in the universe. Failures are human, not divine. When God "fails," as on the cross at Calvary, it is only because the apparent failure is His victory. What a great God! What Paul confirms about our salvation and sanctification in Philippians 1:6 is also true of all that God intends: "[H]e who started a good work in you will carry it on to completion until the day of Christ Jesus." Each and every one of God's purposes is like this.

We must pursue goals God's way, in His time, and at His speed. Humans often tend to accomplish their goals only to look good, to get a promotion at work, or simply to feel good about themselves. But God's purpose is not to look good, which is why Christ did not look good on the cross but did accomplish the divine goal. The purpose or goal of God for each one of His creatures is the praise of His glory, as He has declared in His Word.

The reality is that . . .

- We can accomplish our goals and be outside of God's will.
- We can accomplish our goals and destroy those who are around us.
- We can accomplish our goals even in church without having glorified God.

In our day, the secular world's goal is to have bigger and faster things. This way of thinking has also permeated the life of the believer in such a way that the objective of many pastors is to grow their congregations in order to quickly reach mega-church status; while others seek to plant as many churches as possible in as little time as possible. And while all of this may appear good, that does not mean that it necessarily is. The reality is that numbers have never impressed God. The Lord reduced Gideon's army from 30,000 men to 300 so that it was abundantly clear that He had given them the victory. Henry Blackaby, in his book on spiritual leadership, says: "Churches often use the world's methods to draw a crowd. A grand performance done with excellence, using high-tech sound equipment, professional lighting, eye-catching brochures, and charismatic leadership can draw a crowd. It will not, however, build a church. Only Christ can do that."[3] Numbers do not necessarily please God; it does not matter if there are millions of people or millions of dollars. This is why, in our church, we established as one of our nonnegotiable values the principle that changed lives will be our only measure of success. Remember that a life well-lived is one that is lived for God's glory, and this requires a life of vertical focus.

On one occasion, I had the opportunity to interview Dr. R. C. Sproul in 2016. At the end of the interview, I was able to ask Dr. Sproul if he could summarize the content of our entire conversation in just one phrase or idea so that his words could serve as a final message for all of the leaders in Latin America. These were his words: "Do everything you possibly can in every work that you are involved in for the singular glory of God." In ancient Greek, the word *glory (doxa)* meant "opinion."[4] In the New Testament, that opinion is always good. Therefore, the idea in the New Testament is to exalt the name of God by speaking well of Him. In the same way, as we live for His glory, our life's testimony helps to magnify the image of God before others and to change the idea that many have of Him.

The Goal: Finishing the Race Well

At the end of his days, perhaps weeks or months before his death, the apostle Paul reflects upon how he was finishing the Christian race and writes the following in his Second Letter to Timothy (his youngest disciple): "For I am already being poured out as a drink offering, and the time for my departure is close. I have fought the good fight, I have finished the race, I have kept the faith" (2 Tim. 4:6–7). Paul had nothing more left to do. He had run the race and finished it well. Note how the apostle refers to his death as an offering. For God, it is not only important how we live but also how we die. If we live for God's glory, we should die the same way.

There is a battle to fight in the Christian life, and Paul calls it "the good fight." All along the way, sooner or later, the believer will face temptation, hurt, offense, loss, suffering, and pain, which are all part of what we must live in this fallen world for the glory of God. All of this is part of the battle that we must fight. It is important for us to remember that the Christian life is a race; and what is important is not how we start, but how we finish. Many people have extraordinary testimonies of conversion but

make holy

very poor testimonies of sanctification. So, what good are they? We must run the race well, and God gives us His grace in order that we may do so. It is not simply about finishing; it is finishing well. As such, a life well-lived is that life that begins and ends well. Now, this does not mean that we will not fall along the way. There will certainly be stumbles, and some of these will be significant. As someone said on one occasion: "He who has never failed cannot be great. Failure is the true test of greatness."[5]

Peter had an enormous failure in his life. However, his story doesn't end there. It ends with his being crucified along with his Lord. He got up, fought the good fight, and finished the race well. On the other hand, in the Scriptures we find several individuals who did not finish well, who were eliminated early on along the way. Abimelech, Samson, Absalom, Ahab, and Josiah were people who started well but fell quickly. Eli was another one of these figures who also did not finish well. He went along well for quite some time, but eventually finished poorly. His sons, Hophni and Phinehas, dishonored God; and Eli, although being the high priest, did not judge them as was commanded by the law (Lev. 24:15–16). As a consequence, both of his sons died in battle both on the same day; and when Eli received word that his sons had died and the ark had been captured by the Philistines, he fell backward and died of a broken neck (1 Sam. 4:11, 17–18).

The biblical account shows us how God allowed Eli's life to end in disgrace, as part of divine judgment, and how his two sons died in battle on the same day, also as a part of that same judgment. Likewise, we see how God announces to Eli that practically none of his descendants would reach old age, but that He would spare some of them so that Eli could see them and suffer as part of His judgment. Why? Because Eli did not correct his sons in a timely fashion. In 1 Samuel we find the words of the Lord to Eli:

So sad

> "Therefore, this is the declaration of the LORD,
> the God of Israel: 'I did say that your family and
> your forefather's family would walk before me

forever. But now,' this is the LORD's declaration, 'no longer! For those who honor me I will honor, but those who despise me will be disgraced. Look, the days are coming when I will cut off your strength and the strength of your forefather's family, so that none in your family will reach old age. You will see distress in the place of worship, in spite of all that is good in Israel, and no one in your family will ever again reach old age. Any man from your family I do not cut off from my altar will bring grief and sadness to you. All your descendants will die violently. This will be the sign that will come to you concerning your two sons Hophni and Phinehas: both of them will die on the same day." (1 Sam. 2:30–34)

What a terrible way to end life!

Other people ended up halfway there. David was a man after God's own heart, but even though we cannot say that he finished the race well, we also cannot say that he finished poorly. King David sinned greatly against God and his family; and from there, he truly fell apart. As a result, after having reached its highest point of development under David's reign, the kingdom of Israel began a process of decline that has never since been reversed. As such, this great servant of God did not finish the race in the best way possible.

Nevertheless, there are other people in the Bible who finished well (human beings of flesh and blood just like we are) and were subject to temptation and weakness, but even still, finished well; men like Abraham, Job, Joshua, Caleb, Elijah, Jeremiah, Isaiah, Daniel, Paul, Peter, John, and many more.

Many of us run the Christian race, but in an overly confident manner, with much passion at the start, only to end up losing focus along the way.[6] When this occurs, some within our flock say to us: "Pastor, I do not know what happened to me . . . I remember when I used to teach, preach, evangelize, and sing in the choir," and so on. These people appear to live in the glories of the past. We cannot experience a life well-lived while dwelling on the past, for it no longer exists. We must live in the present.

In his book *Finishing Strong*, Steve Farrar talks about how, in the year 1945, there were three young preachers who had much promise: Billy Graham, Charles Templeton, and Bron Clifford. Some thought that the least promising of those three was Billy Graham. In fact, the young lady whom Billy Graham had fallen in love with accepted his marriage proposal, but some months later broke her engagement with Billy because, according to her, he did not show great promise, so she did not see any true purpose in his life. However, although these men started off the race well, by the year 1950, Templeton had left the ministry and abandoned the faith, saying that he no longer believed in orthodox Christianity. Four years later, Clifford had left his wife and children and had lost his ministry, his health, and finally, his life due to alcoholism.[7] Of the three most famous and promising evangelists of that time, only one finished well. Billy Graham, who went home to be with the Lord in February of 2018, remained a faithful servant of the Lord and was greatly respected both within and outside the Christian arena. Praise the Lord for the faithful life of this man! His children

A life well-lived leaves a mark on others. It is impossible for us to go down in history without leaving some kind of legacy, whether it be in the life of our spouse, our children, our church, or our colleagues, and claim that we have lived well. God created us to bring glory to His name in all that we do. We must leave a legacy of faith that others can imitate and continue to build upon. Now, in order not to run the risk of being misinterpreted, we need to remember that the grace of God and not human wisdom is what enables us to run the race well. God equips us to run it well, but some of us are lazy.

Requirements for Accomplishing Goals

I. A life well-lived needs a close relationship with God.

Christ established this first goal for life: "Love the Lord your God with all your heart, with all your soul, and with all your mind" (Matt. 22:37). A close relationship with God is not the same as having daily devotions, as good as this may be. The formation of the character of Christ in us, along with a display of the fruit of the Spirit and a consistency between what we profess and practice, is the evidence of a close relationship with God. He has always sought after man, but that search only brings benefit to man and not to God. This speaks of how much He loves us. God is complete in Himself from eternity past, but He has sought after man because He knows that the only way in which we will become transformed into His image is if we remain in a close relationship with Him. This reality can be seen throughout biblical history.

God placed man and woman in the garden of Eden, a place which He designed to be beautiful and perfect so that they could have a relationship with Him. We could say that this was the first temple of worship to our God. When the sin of Adam and Eve ruined it, God decided to make a tabernacle in which to dwell amongst His people. There, He descended to the most holy place and allowed sinful men to have a relationship with him through the priest. Later, when the Hebrew people left the wilderness and established a new land, God gave instructions for the construction of a temple where He would dwell. This temple was inaugurated by King Solomon (2 Chron. 6–7). After the revelation through the prophets of the Old Testament, God sent us His Son, in whom the fullness of the Godhead dwelt and dwells. In fact, Christ referred to His body as the temple: "Therefore the Jews said, 'This temple took forty-six years to build, and will you raise it up in three days?' But [Jesus] was speaking about the temple of his body" (John 2:20–21). And when Jesus left this world, the Father and the Son sent the third person of the Trinity, the Holy

Spirit, who came to dwell within each believer. What before was outside, in the most holy place, now came to dwell within human beings. Ultimately, in the New Jerusalem, we will dwell with Jesus, and we will see Him face-to-face, just as He is. It will be as if we had returned to Eden. Adam ceased to live well when he separated himself from God; therefore, if we wish to have a life well-lived, we need to cultivate a close relationship with Him.

2. For a life well-lived, we need a "teachable" character.

A person with a teachable character is one who can learn from others and who allows others to correct him. He is someone who seeks to look to those who have gone before, those who have lived consistently, and those from whom he wishes to know the answers to the questions. In his third letter, John mentions someone who is the opposite of this: "I wrote something to the church, but Diotrephes, who loves to have first place among them, does not receive our authority" (3 John 9). Diotrephes was not teachable, and, therefore, would not finish well. None of us will finish well if we do not have a teachable character. This is why the Word says: "Pride comes before destruction, and an arrogant spirit before a fall" (Prov. 16:18).

3. We need a life centered on fulfilling the purposes of God.

This area is crucial in the Christian life. We have many personal ideals that do not form part of the purposes of God in our lives. This is due to the fact that the majority of Christians have a horizontally oriented life, that is, a life that seeks to fulfill its highest aspirations this side of eternity. But we must not forget what Ephesians 2:10 says: "For we are his workmanship, created in Christ Jesus for good works, which God prepared ahead of time for us to do." Many times, we have performed works that God did not prepare beforehand, and, as He did not prepare them, we should not perform them. Therefore, sooner or later, we will have to return to the works that He prepared for us from eternity past. On occasion, it will be necessary for a great fish to swallow us and later vomit us out on the seashore, such as occurred in the case of Jonah. The ways of God are sovereign, and we all must learn this lesson.

We need to center our life on the purposes of God, as this is what constitutes a life well-lived. It is difficult for us to imagine a life consecrated to the purposes of God but full of dissatisfaction and complaint; we cannot join these two things. God did not create us so that we would complain when things are not going well, but for the praise of His glory. We do not see how complaining can glorify God; it does not reflect Him, does not exalt Him, nor does it cause others to think better of God. And as we have already seen, glorifying God consists of magnifying the image that others have of Him.   *Corrie ten boom*

A life centered on the purposes of God naturally produces satisfaction and joy; and this is what He wants to give us: a life of abundance. Christ said: "I have come so that they may have life and have it in abundance" (John 10:10b).

4. A life well-lived requires a life of faith.

A life of unbelief will produce much instability. Required faith must be placed in the person of Jesus and His Word, which tells us what God is like. We need to trust in His sovereignty and His providence; these two things go hand in hand. The sovereignty of God means that He has the right, the authority, and the power to do whatever He pleases without question. Now, as His character is holy and just, all that He desires will also be holy and just. He has the right because He is the ruler over and owner of heaven and earth. Providence, on the other hand, has to do with the special care that God has for His creation every day, minute by minute, second by second. This also includes us when we speak of the exercise of His rule. We need to trust in the Lord even when the news is bad, as it is part of His sovereign and providential care.

Such a life of faith allowed Paul to be joyful even while in prison because he trusted God's purposes, His sovereignty, and in His love. Can you imagine the emotional and spiritual stability that this should produce? But the only way to live like this is if our life is vertically focused, as we see in the following words of Paul:

> Now I want you to know, brothers and sisters, that what has happened to me has actually advanced the gospel, so that it has become known throughout the whole imperial guard, and to everyone else, that my imprisonment is because I am in Christ. Most of the brothers have gained confidence in the Lord from my imprisonment and dare even more to speak the word fearlessly. (Phil. 1:12–14)

Paul was joyful because, despite being in prison, the gospel continued to advance, and his imprisonment had instilled courage in other believers and encouraged them to share the Word without fear of consequences.

5. A life well-lived requires self-examination.

A life characterized by self-examination is one that pays attention to the warning signs. Because of our deceitful hearts, we are capable of sinning and being unaware of our sin. This was the case with David, who, after committing adultery with Bathsheba and giving the order for her husband to be abandoned on the battlefield to cause his death, took Bathsheba to be his wife. He did this without realizing his sin until the prophet Nathan confronted him about it. Our worst enemy is not outside of us, but within us. We sin and later try to justify our sin by arguing that we made the decision because it was a matter of conscience or conviction. Such could be the case, but frequently what we call conviction is simply rebellion, which is nothing more than adherence to our own convictions while obedience is adherence to biblical convictions.

6. A life well-lived is one of gratefulness.

The Christian affirms that God is good, just, sovereign, and that He orchestrates all things, but later complains when God orchestrates circumstances in his life that he does not like. Ultimately, every complaint goes against God, who either allowed or sent into our lives the circumstance about which we complain. No one expresses this idea better than Moses:

> Moses continued, "The LORD will give you meat to eat this evening and all the bread you want in the morning, for he has heard the complaints that you are raising against him. Who are we? Your complaints are not against us but against the LORD." (Exod. 16:8)

Our grumbling and complaining denies everything that we affirm regarding the character of God. We need a life of gratitude to God and to men. The result will be the absence of complaint. Our lives reveal our true convictions better than our words.

7. Our past must be healed in order for us to have a life well-lived.

Many people are hurt and resentful in the present due to things in their past from which they have never been healed. We cannot move forward if we are still living in the past. Paul understood this concept perfectly and in other context wrote the following:

> Not that I have already reached the goal or am already perfect, but I make every effort to take hold of it because I also have been taken hold of by Christ Jesus. Brothers and sisters, I do not consider myself to have taken hold of it. But one thing I do: Forgetting what is behind and reaching forward to what is ahead, I pursue as my

goal the prize promised by God's heavenly call
in Jesus Christ. (Phil. 3:12–14)

In order to live in such a way that God is glorified through
us, we need to leave behind all hurt, bitterness, relationships that
were toxic and continue to be, sinful habits that we have cultivated, customs that we have acquired, and business that does not
please God. Equally, there are thoughts that we need to change,
possessions that we need to sell or give away, positions we need
to leave behind, passions to bury, disappointments to forget, and
many other things that rob us of the joy of our salvation and,
in some cases, bring consequences to our lives. Brethren, "the
sufferings of this present time are not worth comparing with the
glory that is going to be revealed to us" (Rom. 8:18). Do not forget
this. Our perspective of life determines the quality of life that we
will ultimately have.

Final Reflection

For the vast majority of people, a life well-lived is one filled
with pleasure, travel, and fun. But for the child of God, a life well-
lived consists in having a vertical focus, an eternal perspective
of life, and a continuous pursuit of the glory of God. In the past,
the good life consisted of an intellectually and morally virtuous
life. Therefore, happiness equaled a life of virtue. The successful
person knew how to live well . . . virtuously. At present, however,
the good life is seen as the satisfaction of whatever desire that one
may have. As such, a person is considered to be successful if he
obtains the things that satisfy his longings and desires.

Equally, we can say that we live in the midst of a generation that does not think about the possibility of making sacrifice
for any ideal. Many believers desire the blessings of the apostle
Paul, but we rarely hear of someone saying that he is willing
to live as Paul did. When Adam and Eve began their life, they
had the best life possible, but they were not satisfied because at

some point, the desire to be like God arose in them. From that moment on, they did not have a good life like the one that they had previously enjoyed. What caused this change was a lack of trust in God, a dissatisfaction with what they were, and a lack of gratitude to God for all that He had placed in their hands. These are the same things that today frequently prevent God's children from having a good life.

We live in a fallen world and, therefore, we have to live with correct expectations regarding what to expect from this world on this side of glory. Incorrect expectations have caused great pain and unnecessary suffering for the children of men, including the children of God. As a consequence, life does not give us what we want or hope for. Therefore, in order to have a good life, we need to accept the things that do not turn out as we thought they would or hoped they would at the beginning. Finally, as our God is infinitely good and has also loved us with an infinite love, we should be grateful because no matter how we live, we will always be better than we deserve. In light of this, we have often told our counselees that there are three key words or activities that can reduce the enormous amount of counseling cases in the church, and these three are *expectations* (correct ones), *acceptance*, and *gratitude*.

CHAPTER 8

Be a Servant for His Glory

*Adopt the same attitude as that of Christ Jesus, who,
existing in the form of God, did not consider equality
with God as something to be exploited. Instead he
emptied himself by assuming the form of a servant,
taking on the likeness of humanity. And when he had
come as a man, he humbled himself by becoming obedient
to the point of death—even to death on a cross.*

Philippians 2:5–8

Introduction

The biblical text above forms part of a portion of the
Scriptures that many scholars think made up part of a hymn
sung by the early church and that Paul did not originally write
it, but rather he incorporated it in this letter to the church at
Philippi.[1] This opinion has to do with the rhythm and structure
of the passage. To be sure, we certainly see how the early church
had a very clear idea of the incarnation and glorification of our

Lord. This passage is one of extraordinary beauty and theological depth. For many scholars, it is the core of Paul's letter to the Philippians. In fact, some go beyond that, saying that this passage, traditionally known as the self-humiliation of Christ, is the core of the whole Bible because it explains how much our redemption cost the Son. It cost Him His descent into the world to guarantee our ascent to glory; it cost Him humiliation to guarantee our glorification and death to give us life.

When Christ took our place on the cross, there *He showed us the true spirit of a servant.* A servant for His glory does not live for himself; he knows that his own will, plans, and purposes belong to his Master, as we saw in the previous chapter. The word *servant* used in this passage and in multiple others is the Greek word *doulos.* This word, *doulos*, appears some 124 times in the New Testament[2] and is practically never translated correctly, perhaps because the translators did not want to give the wrong impression with relation to how Christ sees us. The purpose can be reduced to one purpose alone, and that is to please his Master. We believe in all of the Bible there is no text that demonstrates better than Philippians 2:5–8 what the heart of a servant who has given his life to God should be like.

Now, the question is: Why does Paul choose to insert a passage so theological as this one into a letter that has been called the letter of joy and that was meant to encourage the believers of that church in the midst of trial and persecution? We might think that a passage such as this one would perhaps appear in the book of Romans or Hebrews, which are, in theological terms, the two weightiest books in the New Testament. But this is not the case; it appears in the book of Philippians. Why? This is a good question, and we could suggest (or perhaps even speculate) that Paul inserted it here as a response to internal divisions that were occurring amongst the believers in Philippi and that Paul had gotten word of this. About such divisions, he writes:

> I urge Euodia and I urge Syntyche to agree in the
> Lord. Yes, I also ask you, true partner, to help
> these women who have contended for the gospel
> at my side, along with Clement and the rest of
> my coworkers whose names are in the book of
> life. (Phil. 4:2–3)

The apostle maintained contact with the churches he had planted and was concerned about some of the news that he had heard. When hearing of the conflict between Euodia and Syntyche, Paul presents Christ to them as someone to be imitated: His lifestyle, His model of service, and His way of getting along with others. This explains why Paul, before discussing the humiliation of Christ, begins chapter 2 in the following way:

> If, then, there is any encouragement in Christ,
> if any consolation of love, if any fellowship with
> the Spirit, if any affection and mercy, make my
> joy complete by thinking the same way, having
> the same love, united in spirit, intent on one
> purpose. Do nothing out of selfish ambition or
> conceit, but in humility consider others as more
> important than yourselves. Everyone should look
> not to his own interests, but rather to the interests
> of others. (Phil. 2:1–4)

We do not have the time to do a detailed exposition of this biblical text, since our primary focus here is the self-humiliation of Christ; but a quick look at verse 2 gives us Paul's proposal:

- Think the same way . . . This requires humility.
- Have the same love . . . This requires intimate communion with God.
- Be united in spirit . . . This requires spiritual maturity.
- Be intent on one purpose . . . This requires submission of our will to His.

This is the strategy that Paul uses to seal any possible crack that could weaken the body of Christ, and we can easily see it. But the questions, then, are: How do we accomplish this? How do we accomplish thinking the same way, having the same loving, being united in spirit, and being intent on one purpose?

The Self-Humiliation of Christ

The answer to the previous questions about how we accomplish thinking the same way is found in the passage on the self-humiliation of Christ that we are considering. It is preferable to use the term self-humiliation, because this was a voluntary act that our Lord carried out. Pharaoh was humbled by God; Nebuchadnezzar was humbled by God; and Jonah, also, was humbled by God. The human heart is rebellious and must be subdued, but Christ was not humbled by anyone. He humbled Himself. We rarely experience self-humiliation. It is most often the case that God has to subdue our will. Our ego is larger than our will; and, as such, for many of us, the most important thing is to ensure that we keep our position of prevalence, although, in the end, we lose. But we lose when we refuse to bend our will, and this is what characterizes rebellion. This was the spirit of Cain, who argued with God when he was reprimanded for the offering he presented to the Lord.

Recently, a missionary gave an account of an occurrence that illustrates in a certain way what we are trying to establish here. On one occasion, this missionary saw how two strong and powerful mountain goats were walking from the opposite direction toward one another and met head-on while traveling down a passageway connecting two mountains. The path was extremely narrow, and only one goat could pass at a time. Given the narrowness of the path, they also could not turn around to head back from where they came. On each side of them was a very dangerous drop-off. Instead of fighting each other and risking their lives, at one point, one of the two goats hunched over and allowed the other goat to jump over it. This is a good example of what it means to have the correct attitude in seeking to consider others better than ourselves.

Sadly, we rarely have the attitude of these two goats; we prefer to butt heads over yielding to each other. In nature itself, God teaches us how a servant's attitude should be. So Paul, knowing how rebellious the heart of man is and having heard of something that was occurring in the church at Philippi, wrote to them and said:

> Adopt the same attitude as that of Christ Jesus, who, existing in the form of God, did not consider equality with God as something to be exploited. Instead he emptied himself by assuming the form of a servant, taking on the likeness of humanity. And when he had come as a man, he humbled himself by becoming obedient to the point of death—even death on a cross. (Phil. 2:5–8)

These verses present the best model of a servant that has been written in more than two thousand years of history and the best strategy to prevent the enemy from wreaking havoc among us. This text has no parallel in redemptive history. God the Creator gave up all of His privileges to give His life for rebels who needed to become worshipers.

Someone once said: "If you want to find out what a worker is really like, don't give him responsibilities—give him privileges."[3] This person explained that, with money, we can get someone to carry out his responsibilities appropriately; but only a true servant knows how to handle privileges properly. A typical leader, like we have seen in the secular world and even in the church of Christ, will use his privileges to promote himself; but a servant will use his privileges to further the cause of the kingdom.

If a true servant does not use his privileges to benefit himself but rather to advance the kingdom, then it is clearly evident that no one has been a better servant than our Lord Jesus Christ. No one else has handled privileges like He has. No one else has handled power, position, authority, the knowledge He had of others, and the temptations He had as a man the way that Christ did.

The Attitude that Was in Christ Jesus

In the original text, the Greek word for "attitude" (*phroneo*) refers more so to the way of thinking, to the natural inclination of our thoughts. This is why in many translations of the Bible the text of Philippians 2:5 says: "Have this *mind* among yourselves, which is yours in Christ Jesus" (ESV, emphasis added). The Lord Jesus, before taking on human flesh, had *a mental attitude, a willingness of spirit, and a natural inclination* that we usually do not have and which allowed Him to consider the mission that would be given to Him. Before we carry out a mission with God, He has to form in us our own mental attitude of being a servant (being before doing). Now, I would like for us to use a technicality for a moment, which will then be explained in a straightforward way. The expression, "Have this same mind," is in the present tense, the imperative mode, and the active voice. This may sound a bit complicated, but it is extremely simple and helps us to understand some of the things that we are trying to emphasize. The fact that this expression is in the present tense helps us to understand that Paul is calling us to have an attitude or way of thinking which is similar to that of Jesus, but in a continuous way; we should assume this way of thinking as a lifestyle. It is not like we are going to have this attitude today only to have a different one tomorrow. No! Absolutely not. The attitude of Christ should be our style of life, according to the text. God does not call us only to behave like a servant, because that can change from time to time. He calls us to *be* servants and not just to act like servants intermittently, which is what we often see and do.

The active voice of the verb just mentioned demonstrates that it is a personal decision that requires an act of the will. We are not passively transformed into servants. Not at all! This transformation requires our participation. We must decide against the desires of the flesh in order to please our God, and we must not wait until we have the desire to do it, as is often the case. The lack of an attitude of service in us obeys our rebellious condition, which we frequently admit when listening to sermons, reading books and articles, or in personal conversations, but we do not change. God has to form in us a heart of service, and there is no better place to do this than in the desert. But at the same time, we must make a decision. Where does God's sovereignty come together with man's will? The answer to that question is beyond our comprehension, but the Bible affirms both.

And to complete the idea that the verb is in the imperative mode implies that Paul is not making a suggestion or giving a simple opinion, but that, in his apostolic authority, he is ordering the Philippians to continually adopt as a pattern of living the way of thinking or the attitude that was in Christ Jesus when He decided to take on human flesh. God has to transform us into servants because we are born rebels, but Christ, from eternity past, was the great servant because he offered up Himself as the Lamb who was slain. It is one thing to be born to serve as Christ was, but having to be transformed into a servant is something very distinct. The disciples had to be transformed into servants, and the lives of Peter, John, James, and Paul are good illustrations of this reality. Kent Hughes, in his commentary on Philippians, quotes the poet Robert Raines, who wrote the following lines while thinking on that occasion when James and John argued about sitting at the right hand and left hand of Christ when He entered into His kingdom:

> I am like James and John
> Lord, I size up other people
> in terms of what they can do for me;
> how they can further my program,
> feed my ego,

satisfy my needs,
give me strategic advantage.
I will exploit people,
ostensibly for your sake,
but really for my own sake.
Lord, I turn to you
to get the inside track
and obtain special favors,
your direction for my schemes,
your power for my projects,
your sanction for my ambitions,
your blank checks for whatever I want.
I am like James and John.[4]

We are like James and John, which is why we need this model offered to us by the apostle Paul in Philippians 2.

He Emptied Himself of His Glory

Before His incarnation, Christ existed in the form of God or existed as God from eternity past and will continue to exist as God because, by definition, He cannot vary in His existence. God is immutable. The word translated in Philippians 2:6 as "form" is *morphe* in Greek which, according to scholars, is a word that speaks of the external expression of an internal reality, which means that Christ existed as God in His very essence from all eternity past. John 1:1 affirms this principle that Jesus was God from eternity past. The incarnation of Christ has a special character, as the mere fact that God became man, even without anything else occurring, involves an extraordinary act of humility. The eternal God that cannot even be contained by the heavens who exists outside of time and space came into this temporal world to share humanity with man. He of whom Job said "the heavens are not pure in his sight" (Job 15:15b) would now have to live amongst extremely sinful men. This is a remarkable example of the divinity of God.

The humiliation of Christ has nothing to do with ours. He began as Creator; we begin as creatures. He began as Lord and we as slaves. He began as exalted and we as fallen and corrupt creatures who have darkened minds, hearts of flesh, and rebellious and prideful minds which are imprisoned by sin. Everything related to this condition is worthy of being humiliated, but not Christ, the Messiah and Redeemer, He who is holy, holy, holy and whose eyes are so pure that they cannot even look upon sin. This was the condition in which Christ existed from all eternity, and despite being exalted, He became a servant.

The Son enjoyed the purity of the kingdom of the heaven, the worship of the angels and archangels, and servants who were joyful in serving Him. He descended in position, but not in essence or nature because He never ceased being the true God, nor did He cease having the same nature as the Father.

We already mentioned that the best way to know what someone truly is like is by observing how he handles his privileges. If this is the case, then the example of servanthood that Christ gave us is unsurpassed because no other being has ever had more power, more authority, more privileges, and more knowledge available to him than the person of Jesus. And having all of this, it is He who humbled Himself.

Jesus . . .

- with all the power in the universe at His disposal, allowed Himself to be nailed to a cross;
- with an authority so great that even the winds obeyed him, submitted Himself to the corrupt authority of men;
- with all of the privileges typical of divinity, emptied Himself of them and did not reclaim them; and

- with all of the knowledge of the heart of men, entrusted His mission to twelve untrustworthy men, who would deny Him at the end of His life.

Why? Because He lived as *a servant for the glory of God.* We must have the heart of a true servant in order to handle the privileges that the Master grants us.

The Self-Renunciation of Christ

The text of Philippians says that Christ emptied Himself. Note how God the Father is not the one who empties Christ; rather, He empties Himself. This was a voluntary act motivated by the glory of the Father's name. Now, of what did Christ empty Himself? At the end of the nineteenth century, some Methodist theologians began to create the theory of the *kenosis,* which asserts that, by becoming incarnate, Christ emptied Himself of some attributes which included His omnipresence, His omnipotence, and His omniscience, which is impossible. God cannot set aside His attributes and continue being God. He defines Himself as immutable in Malachi 3:6, and in James 1:17 we are told that in God "does not change like shifting shadows."

When the text states that Christ emptied Himself, it is not talking about setting aside some of His divine attributes, rather setting aside the glory that He shared with the Father from all eternity. This is why on the night before fulfilling His mission, Christ prayed to the Father saying, "Now, Father, glorify me in your presence with that glory I had with you before the world existed" (John 17:5). He set aside His glory; He set aside the worship offered to Him by the heavenly beings; He set aside His rights and prerogatives to come and represent to men the true God and true man. During His incarnation, Christ voluntarily decided not to make use of some of these attributes, but He still possessed them. The second person of the Trinity did not cling to His divine condition, which would have been perfectly understandable. Why set aside a position of privilege such as this to come down to those who would not know how to appreciate His act of abandon and surrender? This is what makes His giving up all of this so extraordinary. This is the attitude, the mind, that was in Christ Jesus that we must adopt if we truly want to be *a servant for His glory.*

Why was the Creator so willing to surrender his prerogatives, rights, and privileges, and, yet, the creature is so reluctant? The answer is not complicated. The creature does not yield to his prerogatives, rights, and positions because these fleeting things are those that incorrectly give him value. So, we wield and hold on to them. The servant who finds his value in the things of this temporal world cannot serve for the glory of God. Servants for His glory have only one concern: what they do to reflect the character of their Master. Once we are secure in God, it becomes much easier for us to let go of those things in which we had placed our trust. When this occurs, God must empty us of many things in life. This differs from the way Christ, who emptied Himself, did it, recognizing that His value was not in what He possessed, but in what He really was. We claim as our own that which is not truly ours. But Christ claimed nothing despite the fact that everything belonged to Him. Jesus let go of what was His, while we grasp at what belongs to God. We say that He is the Master of heaven and earth, but we act like we are the true masters, even thinking that we are our own masters and masters over everyone else because we are controlling. The disciples had to learn to surrender control and we must also learn to do so. In Mark 9:38–40 we read:

> John said to him, "Teacher, we saw someone driving out demons in your name, and we tried to stop him because he wasn't following us."
>
> "Don't stop him," said Jesus, "because there is no one who will perform a miracle in my name who can soon afterward speak evil of me. For whoever is not against us is for us."

The disciples had our same syndrome of wanting to control everything. We are not the owners of the ministry. God is the owner of the ministry. Warren Wiersbe, in his book *On Being a Servant of God*, says that "ministry takes place when divine resources meet human needs through loving channels to the glory of God."[5] This helps us to understand that the ministry is not ours because it takes place when divine resources meet human needs. Wiersbe is correct; when it comes to ministry, we are all bankrupt because we do not have the resources necessary to minister to the human soul. We do not have resources, but we act as if we did; we give glory to God, but we want the credit for ourselves. Steve Brown, author, seminary professor, and teacher at Key Life ministries, has a very distinct way of putting things, and on one occasion, in a letter that he had sent to his followers and that we had the opportunity to read some time ago, said: "often, we are so critical of ourselves that we feel like rubbish, but on many other occasions we come to believe that God should make a space for us to occupy the fourth place within the Trinity." We forget that all is of Him, through Him, and to Him (Rom. 11:36). We have nothing, which is why we hold onto everything in effort to take control of what is not ours. But Christ, having everything, gave it up and was left with nothing. Such was His attitude.

We do not relinquish like Christ did because as creatures we are selfish, and in our selfishness, we do not think of others; and if we did, it would not be to consider them as more important than ourselves. We are fearful, selfish, and rebellious. This is why we do not relinquish our rights, positions, opinions, or privileges. All of these things make us feel important and giving them up would be like yielding our sense of importance. The creature will never be willing to give up being the center of attention. When the lights are on, we want them to be on us. We may not say so, but we want it that way. And when the lights are not on us, we do not want them to be on others. We are like the dog in the manger who neither eats nor allows others to eat.

On the contrary, when Jesus took on flesh, His desire was that the light would always be shining on the Father, recognizing and affirming that He was the greatest of all. This explains why Jesus says: "Father, the hour has come. Glorify your Son so that the Son may glorify you" (John 17:1b). The Son's attention was always on others: on God the Father, on the hungry, on hurting people like the Samaritan woman or the prostitute, on the blind. But it was never on Himself. *This is a servant for His glory.*

Christ's attitude of self-sacrifice did not begin after He took on flesh, but before. It began in heaven when He was equal with God and, in that moment, He emptied Himself. When Paul speaks of the mind and attitude that was in Christ, he is referring in part to His willingness to surrender and sacrifice while also speaking of His willingness to come down and humble Himself to the point of death.

For us, upward is better, but for Jesus, downward is the way up to heaven. In our society, the idea of going down or lowering ourselves is rejected; it sounds like something derogatory or unworthy of us. One of the worst offenses for human beings is to be moved from a higher position to a lower one. But Jesus understood that the way to glorify the Father as a servant was to descend and rescue humanity, whose redemption would reflect the glory of the grace of our God.

The Self-Denial of Christ in Serving

Christ took on the "form of a servant, taking on the likeness of humanity" (Phil. 2:7b). When He left heaven, He did so to take on flesh, but in doing this, He not only became man, but also a servant. Jesus could have come down as the head of the Roman Empire, but He did not. When He became flesh, Jesus did not arrive in Athens or Rome, or even Jerusalem, but in Bethlehem, an obscure Middle Eastern village. He went from the company of angels, archangels, cherubim, and seraphim to the company of animals and rural pastors. True servants do not need highly important people at their side in order to have significance. *A servant for His glory* is satisfied in God. Christ took on flesh and became a *doulos*, which translated, means servant. He owed all of Himself to His Master. The will of the *doulos* was the will of his master; his plans and purposes were the exact same as those of his master, as we stated at the beginning. *This is a servant for His glory.*

Someone once said that the greatness of man is not in how many people are under him, but in how many people he serves. Jesus served . . .

- His disciples
- Prostitutes
- Publicans
- Tax collectors and even
- A traitor

The Lord Jesus taught His disciples many things, but on one occasion He stopped to emphasize something regarding His character that they should learn and spoke these words: "[L]earn from me, because I am lowly and humble in heart" (Matt. 11:29b). Humility is a quality that we should learn directly from the Lord. He is the ultimate example of humility. On the contrary, we need to learn to be humble, and the following words from Robert Murray M'Cheyne, delivered in 1840, can help us to understand the importance of Jesus' invitation: "Your . . . sermon lasts an hour or two—your life preaches all the week."[6] When the sheep of our flock observe us throughout the week, what is the sermon that they are listening to, one preached by a humble servant, or one preached by a prideful servant?

This quality of humility that Christ wanted His disciples to learn from Him tends to elude everyone, especially those of us who are leaders. This is partly because the leader has been endowed with gifts, talents, and a calling that often leads him down the road of success. Such success is fertile ground for pride. Therefore, we can say that pride makes humility difficult.

Humility is difficult to harvest, especially in those of us who are leaders of God's people because we often carry out sacred functions:

- We preach a sermon on the holy Word;
- We marry a couple in the presence of God;
- We bury a person who has passed on to the kingdom of heaven; and
- We counsel another through the revelation of God.

As a result, we grow accustomed to handling the sacred until the holy becomes ordinary, and when the sacred turns into the normal, routine, daily, and common, we who are truly ordinary begin to feel extraordinary in our own eyes. Occasionally, we forget how little sacred we are in reality. As such, we need to continually remember how undeserved the privilege is of pastoring the sheep whom Christ has purchased with His blood.

Final Reflection

Given all the above, the paradox of Christ's sacrifice is evident. Let us meditate on the following realities:

- God took on flesh and died in man's place.
- The giver of life lost His life.
- The innocent died in the place of the guilty.
- The judge took the place of the accused.
- The Holy One was made a curse.
- The King dressed in glory was naked on a cross.
- The Lord became a servant.

The Son did all of this for the glory of His father. *This is a servant for His glory.*

Because of this, when the servant understands and accepts the fact that his mission in life has been reduced to one single thing, the glory of his God, from that moment on, he is willing to give his life. Our problem is that we still value our lives too much. In Revelation 12:11, we read about people who "conquered him by the blood of the Lamb and by the word of their testimony; for they did not love their lives to the point of death."

When He took on flesh, Jesus defined His mission, saying that "the Son of Man did not come to be served, but to serve" (Matt. 20:28a) . . . up to the cross. And He accomplished this. How did He do it? By exercising humility, offering Himself to be broken in dependence on His Father and in complete obedience:

- His *humility* allowed Him to relinquish His position.
- His *dependence* on the Father gave Him strength.
- His absolute *obedience* allowed Him to resist every temptation.
- His willingness to be *broken* made it possible for Him to pay for our sins.

These four characteristics define the profile of a servant for His glory: humility, dependence, obedience, and brokenness. These four qualities led Christ to the cross. In closing, there are three things that we cannot forget:

1. We exist for the sake of the kingdom, and the kingdom exists for the sake of the King.
2. We belong to the community of the towel and basin. This is the only community that brings glory to its Lord.
3. If there is to be any blessing, there first has to be brokenness.

This is a servant for His glory.

CHAPTER 9

Be a Spiritual Servant

"A disciple is not above his teacher,
but everyone who is fully trained will be like his teacher."
Luke 6:40

Introduction

Over the last few years, much has been said about leadership; hundreds of books have been published about the topic over the last thirty years. In our view, whenever we see a proliferation of Christian or secular literature on a particular topic, we can assume with some degree of certainty that the increase in publications is usually accompanied by a significant number of conferences and seminars. This is because a crisis has been identified and everyone is making an effort to solve it with their own contribution. At the end of the twentieth century these new books and conferences began to appear, focusing on the topic of leadership, both from a Christian and secular perspective. And we mention this from the beginning because the concept of a spiritual leader is very distant from the natural leader that we frequently see in society. Without a doubt, there are principles of leadership that can find their application both within and outside the church, but the reality is that the essence we possess differs enormously from person to person.

Spiritual leadership has to do with a calling and equipping that God does in a person to carry out a specific task related to the expansion of the kingdom of heaven here on earth. The natural leader seeks to expand his own kingdom or the kingdom of the institution for which he works. The first type or style of leadership is centered on God and the other is centered on the human being. The natural leadership that we see in society tends to exalt the gifts and talents of the person "in charge"; spiritual leadership seeks to exalt the giver of gifts, talents, and opportunities, that is, God.

As the purpose of this introductory section is not to establish from the beginning all of the existing differences between these two types of leadership, let us return once again to that idea that we live in the midst of a crisis in the twenty-first century, which began in the last decades of the previous century. The current crisis is widespread; we see it in the family environment, governments, businesses, and churches. This forces us to ask ourselves: What has caused this crisis? The answer is complex, and we do not intend to dedicate just a few lines to it, but what we can affirm is that together with this leadership crisis is a value crisis that goes hand in hand with it. If there are no leaders who model, there will be no values to teach, which is akin to the story of the chicken and the egg: Which came first, the values crisis or the leadership crisis? We believe that the two have gone hand in hand since the beginning.

The Leadership Crisis

The values and leadership crisis is widespread. And as always occurs, the church has not escaped its ravages, unfortunately. We have to admit it or we will have no hope of change. The reality is that there is not even one area of society that has not been affected by this leadership crisis.

Today, we can see in the nations of the Western world how governments have begun to fill their highest positions of leadership with women, which is basically a reflection of the void in leadership that men have left as well as the poor governments that men have formed in previous years. In stating this, we do not deny the great capabilities that some women possess, as in the case of Margaret Thatcher, the prime minister of the United Kingdom (1979–1990). But we do want to point out that the crisis in which we find ourselves is largely due to a void left by a lack of leadership on the part of many men. Wherever there is a void, someone will fill that void, and this has occurred. Something similar happens in the family environment, of which many are led by wives more so than by husbands. This tendency has continued to produce its own bad fruit because God made man the head of the home, and if man abdicates the position given to him by God, it is only logical to assume that the family nucleus will suffer the consequences.

- According to the U.S. Department of Health and Human Services, National Center for Health Statistics, fatherless children are at a dramatically greater risk of drug and alcohol abuse, mental illness, suicide, poor educational performance, and criminality.
- Over half of all children living with a single mother are living in poverty, a rate five to six times that of kids living with both parents.
- Sixty-three percent of youth suicides are from fatherless homes, according to the U.S. Census Bureau.
- Seventy-two percent of adolescent murderers grew up without fathers. Sixty percent of America's rapists grew up the same way,

according to a study by D. Cornell (et al.), in
Behavioral Sciences and Law.

- Seventy-one percent of all high school dropouts
  come from fatherless homes, according to the
  National Principals Association Report on the
  State of High Schools.
- Eighty percent of rapists motivated with dis-
  placed anger come from fatherless homes
  according to a report in *Criminal Justice and
  Behavior.*
- Ninety percent of all homeless and runaway
  children are from fatherless homes.
- Eighty-five percent of all children that exhibit
  behavioral disorders come from fatherless
  homes, according to a study by the Center for
  Disease Control.[1]

In the church environment, there is a leadership crisis on
every continent. One of the reasons, but not the only one, is that
despite the fact that it has been said that leaders are born and not
made, there is no doubt that leaders also should be formed, and
this has not occurred. No one is born with a book of instructions
in his hand in order to learn how to lead. On the other hand,
the assumption is often made that the position given to a person
comes with the understanding of that position, but this has never
been the case, especially when it comes to leadership. There has
been little training, both in the church and in the secular world,
on how a leader should be.

The leadership crisis is profound because the absence of
values in postmodern society has caused a character crisis in
our day. There is no character without values, and there is no
leadership without character. The absence of values has caused
an absence of character in the individual. Someone once said
that leaders intentionally need to pursue character formation,
because character is not something that is formed naturally, by
osmosis, as is the case with the deformation of character when

we are exposed to bad influences. Hence, Paul warned us: "Bad company corrupts good morals" (1 Cor. 15:33). If we begin to interact frequently and closely with the wrong kind of people, we will naturally and easily become spiritually deformed due to our sinful nature.

Success is a threat to the character of people. The higher we climb the ladder of success, the more the burden of responsibility increases. If character and success are not developed together, then the successful person will end up crushed under the weight of new responsibilities.

Something that has made our current situation even worse is that we live in a society with an accelerated pace of life. Therefore, those whom God has led into a position of leadership say that they do not have time to train disciples. The issue at hand is that if there is no time to train disciples, leadership is not being passed on to the next generation. This was not the model of Jesus, who dedicated time to train and form His disciples. Christ did not start forming His church before the disciples were adequately trained. On the other hand, the accelerated pace of life in which we live has led institutions to place increasingly younger people in positions of leadership. Thus, we see that positions once held by people from forty to fifty years old are now held by people from thirty to forty years old. Perhaps the academic training of today is much better than that of previous generations. But when it comes to leadership, academia is not the only important factor, but also the maturity of the individual.

If we consider the local church, we could say that its leadership is the basis of the organization, so it is imperative for said leadership to be formed before the church is even planted or in its early stages of formation. If we think about families, we would have to affirm that they cannot have any form of stability if there is no head to lead its members. If we consider governments, undoubtedly, we certainly could not have a stable and prosperous nation if its leadership does not possess what is necessary to lead the nation toward its destiny.

All of this is even more important if we consider the times in which we live. Today's generation does not live with a sense of purpose, and when individuals of today's generation do have purpose, these purposes are related to the here and now. If there is anything required to be a leader, in the best sense of the word, it is possessing a purpose greater than the person; and God gives this purpose. If it comes from God, the leader's purpose and vision are supposed to outlive the leader. The people of Israel saw the death of Moses, but the purpose and vision continued in the life of Joshua. When something comes from God, it cannot die with the leader; if it does, we can assume that it did not come from our Lord. Thus, when we think of leadership, there has to be a purpose that is greater than the leader and that can continue on after the leader passes away.

The Importance of Spiritual Leadership

In the gospel of Luke, we see the importance that leadership can be formed and passed on: "A disciple is not above his teacher, but everyone who is fully trained will be like his teacher" (Luke 6:40). This phrase implicitly lets us see that, in Jesus' mind, His church would be developed on the premise of a teacher who would form disciples who would, in turn, form other disciples until the Lord returned. With the following words, Paul instructed Timothy to follow this pattern: "What you have heard from me in the presence of many witnesses, commit to faithful men who will be able to teach others also" (2 Tim. 2:2). The quality of the disciple will depend upon the teaching that is shared with him (the Word), the resemblance of the teacher to the teaching that is given (consistency), and the amount of time that the teacher and disciple spend together.

If the teacher is not concerned with living according to the Word and forming his followers well, he will replicate the same shortcomings as his disciples. Christ wanted His disciples to model His image accurately because the disciples who would come after would be formed in the image of them. The responsibility of the spiritual leader is monumental, as we see in these words of Paul to the Corinthians: "Imitate me, as I also imitate Christ" (1 Cor. 11:1).

John Maxwell has written much on the topic of leadership, and although I do not necessarily agree with all of his theology, I do acknowledge that in the area of leadership there is much of what he teaches that has significant weight and value. One of his many phrases on leadership states: "everything rises and falls on leadership."[2] There is nothing truer. In fact, in the church which I have the privilege of pastoring, each time we have identified problems at the level of the congregation, the leadership has sat down first to examine those areas in our own lives prior to going before the congregation in general, because frequently congregational problems are nothing more than reflections of the problems in leadership. This does not mean that each problem that we encounter in a person is related to a problem within the leadership. Now, if the body of Christ is suffering from a certain sin, it is very likely that the cause lies in the leadership of the body. Sometimes, the problem is in the lack of teaching in a particular area; while other times, it lies in poor practice or inconsistencies on the part of the leadership.

Maxwell also says that "leaders cannot rise above the limitations of their character."[3] Therefore, an organization also will not rise above its leadership. In other words, when it comes to churches, the congregation will only go as far as the leadership in its spiritual and moral development. But if we are talking about the family of those leaders, the children will only go as far as the leader (at least until they begin to establish their independence), and the marriage will only go that far, as well. In this way, our marriage will not surpass our spiritual development; that is impossible. If it is some other institution, it will only go as far as you do. The one who leads is the one who pulls the ones behind him, and he will determine how far they all go. As an application, we also can say that the health and growth of the church are related with the health and growth of the leadership of the church. Therefore, the major challenge for the spiritual leader, in my opinion, is continued growth. When the leadership becomes stagnant, the family, church, or institution becomes stagnant.

The Difference Between Spiritual Leadership and Secular Leadership

When leadership is spoken of in society, its effectiveness is greatly measured by its productivity: "What a great leader; look at how productive he is; look at how many tasks he completed this year." Spiritual leadership is not measured this way, in the least. It is fruitful and does have goals, but its efficiency and effectiveness are measured through the lens of heaven, with Christ and His cause in mind. Spiritual leadership has more to do with being than with doing. Christ did not send the disciples to do anything for the kingdom until He had spent two to three years forming them into men committed to the cause of the kingdom. They were not ready for such a feat until after the death and resurrection of the Lord. One thing is what we are, and another is what the world thinks we are. What we are is our character; what others think we are is our reputation. So many people have not had a good reputation, but character. But God is interested in the character of the individual, in the heart of the person. Therefore, one of the characteristics of a good spiritual leader is that he does not demand from others something that he has not already given or done first. Christ first washed the disciples' feet and later said to them: "'So if I, your Lord and Teacher, have washed your feet, you also ought to wash one another's feet. For I have given you an example, that you also should do just as I have done for you" (John 13:14–15).

We should not demand of others what we cannot first model in our lives because others will immediately observe the dichotomy that exists between what we teach and what we live. Leaders live in glass houses, under constant scrutiny from others. This is true of leadership in general, but it is especially true of those of us who are spiritual leaders.

As we lead God's people, we must remember that He wants to do something through us; this is why He has chosen us. But at the same time, He wants to do something in us. God is continually forming us as we seek to form others. We are not a finished product; rather, we are far from it. The apostle Paul understood this concept perfectly well when he wrote: "Not that I have already reached the goal or am already perfect, but I make every effort to take hold of it because I also have been taken hold of by Christ Jesus" (Phil. 3:12).

Therefore, part of what God will do is to continue to form us through the trials and challenges that He will bring to us or our position through the crises that we must face. God continually kept Moses in crises, but He was molding and shaping him. We must see ourselves as a sheep in formation; the sheep in a church are not just the people who attend, the pastor or pastors are also sheep of Christ's fold, with needs that are often similar to those of everyone else. They are sheep that God is pastoring and forming, still giving them His image, and He will continue doing so until the end of our days.

Definition of Leadership

There does not exist just one definition of leadership; rather, hundreds of distinct definitions have been identified. Some of them correspond to natural or secular leadership and others to spiritual leadership. Let us not forget that we can be excellent leaders in society but terrible leaders in the church. In fact, many churches have committed the error of placing in leadership positions those individuals who occupy similar positions outside of the church without considering the biblical pattern and later have had to deal with the consequences of such decisions. Spiritual and secular leadership respond to two completely different patterns of thought and two totally distinct value systems. Therefore, despite the things that they have in common, these leaders are the fruit of two totally opposed worldviews of leadership.

Someone once defined leadership as "a process whereby an individual influences a group of individuals to achieve a common goal."[4] In this definition, it is good to highlight the word *influences*. Later, we will come back to this word. With this definition in mind, let us now look at what Christ did when He called His first disciples: "'Follow me,' he told them, 'and I will make you fish for people.' Immediately they left their nets and followed him'" (Matt. 4:19–20). Without a doubt, Christ was able to influence a group of individuals to follow Him and do something; and He continues to do so today.

One of Napoleon Bonaparte's observations about the leadership of Christ was precisely that he (Bonaparte) could get his soldiers to follow him when he gave an order while he was alive, but if he died or lost his rank, he could never again get anyone to follow him. Nevertheless, Napoleon noted that Jesus, hundreds of years after His death, continued to influence humanity to follow Him. This is why Bonaparte said that Jesus is the greatest example of leadership that has ever existed.

This should not surprise us given the investiture of Jesus, but it is good to see how even the secular world is able to recognize in a peculiar way those things that we are discussing now.

Oswald Sanders, in his book *Spiritual Leadership*, expressed that "leadership is influence, the ability of one person to influence others to follow his or her lead."[5] Without a doubt, a true leader is capable of getting others to follow him by influence and not imposition. We see that after Jesus' death the people who had been around Him noted that those who had been in His presence were influenced by Him.

Take note of how the following words from the book of Acts put it: "When they observed the boldness of Peter and John and realized that they were uneducated and untrained men, they were amazed and recognized that they had been with Jesus"

(Acts 4:13). People from the secular world saw men who had lived in such a way that when they reacted, they recognized that they had spent time with Jesus. The text says that they were amazed. What amazed them? Peter and John were able to do things that they could not have done due to their lack of academic formation, and they were able to associate the ability of these men with the time that they had spent with the Master. We can indirectly see that Jesus was able to influence these people in an extraordinary way, an influence that was notable even after His death.

Other noteworthy definitions of spiritual leadership are the following:

> Influencing a specific group of people toward God's purposes for the group.[6]

> Moving people from where they are to where God wants them to be.[7]

These are the best definitions of leadership because they allow us to clearly see that a true spiritual leader will move people according to the plans and purposes of God, which will require him continually to depend on the Spirit of God and to find people where they are, in a spiritual sense. Then, this leader will know where God wants him to move the people he is leading, whether they are his children, his disciples, or his employees. This reminds us that the spiritual leader is not autonomous; he is a man under authority, who must give an account to God of what he is doing with the people whom Christ purchased with His blood. In order to know where people are in their walk with God, it is necessary to spend time with them until the leader smells like a sheep, in the case of the church, or until his followers have developed a passion to follow Christ, which can be applied to whichever environment in the Christian life, whether at home or in society.

People or individuals do not always wish to move from where they are to where God wants them to be. We observed this with the children of Israel in the wilderness. But if God has called someone to lead, he will find God's approval and favor resting upon him and will convince the people of the need to move in the direction of God. Some could point out that, during their time wandering through the wilderness, many Israelites refused to follow Moses, and this is true. The biblical account shows how they suffered the consequences, such that the leader is vindicated.

When we read about what spiritual leadership involves, we come across words such as *persuade, prompt, convince, influence, motivate,* and *encourage*; but we do not see words like *impose, force, order,* or *command* as in the case of a boss. It is one thing to be a leader and another to be a boss. Earlier while speaking of leadership, we mentioned the word *purpose*, such that leadership is not exercised blindly or enticingly, as many have sought to do. The leader must have a clear idea of his vision, that is, where he is going. If you do not know where you are going, you will not be able to persuade others to follow you. Leadership is not like the classic example of a bus driver who stops at the station and someone asks him: "Where are you going, driver?" And he responds, "I do not know, but get on!" No one boards a bus without knowing where it is going.

We have discussed two definitions of leadership, one well-summarized and the other more extensive, which allows us to talk about some of the intrinsic aspects of spiritual leadership. Here is the short definition: *"leadership is the ability to motivate others to follow our example."* This definition is inspired by the words of Paul in 1 Corinthians 11:1, where he literally says: "Imitate me, as I also imitate Christ." One must be very sure of his own testimony to dare to write something similar. Thinking about this definition helps us because it reminds us that our walk should be an example that others can imitate. This calls us to reflection and soul-searching. Finally, let us review another definition of spiritual leadership that we examined earlier because there are fundamental aspects of leadership that we have not yet considered. Sadly, this last definition is much more extensive than the previous ones, and it will lead us to reflect on some areas that we have not ventured into yet.

> Leadership is the ability of a person who has been chosen and prepared by God to motivate others to imitate his example, even to the extent of paying whatever price is necessary to achieve the goal that God has set before him.

Now we can see that the spiritual leader is not someone who gets up one day and says, "I want to be a leader tomorrow"; rather, he is someone whom God has trained for such a function. In fact, according to the Word of God, leadership is a gift. In Romans 12, we find different types of gifts, and in verse 8 we are exhorted that the one who has the gift of leading should do it with diligence. In this definition, we can see that the spiritual leader should be someone chosen by God to carry out His purposes. And God does not only choose, He also prepares him to motivate others to imitate his example. Although Jesus is our example, there is no doubt that God has given us parents in the case of children, husbands in the case of wives, and pastors in the case of churches, to model and motivate those who follow behind. Another thing that we must accomplish is to convince ourselves that in leadership, there is a price to pay, just as this last definition mentions. As has always been said, the leader should be willing to arrive earlier and stay later than any other person. Therefore, the leader cannot think about living by the same standard as the sheep.

We know that God's standard is perfection, and no one will reach it on this side of glory, but at the same time, we must recognize that within the flock of God, the sheep are at different levels of sanctification. For this reason, it is the leader's responsibility to model the standard that is above the standard of the sheep. The leader, no matter his position of leadership, is just another sheep in God's fold, but he is not simply a sheep. He is someone who goes ahead, guiding and protecting the sheep from falling before the temptations of the world. But this leader can never forget that the world is not the only stumbling block for the sheep. This is why Paul says that if eating meat is a stumbling block for someone, the leader is willing to sacrifice himself and never eat meat so as not to cause his brother to stumble (1 Cor. 8:13).

The Bible does not reveal the extent to which Paul would claim that "the leader must be careful to walk not only before God but also before men." In the last few years, the church has allowed itself to be fooled into thinking that the only important thing is to judge the intentions of the heart, as if this were the only thing that God judges. This way of thinking is not in line with the Word. The apostle Paul lets us clearly see what is the truth behind this principle: "Indeed, we are giving careful thought to do what is right, not only before the Lord but also before people" (2 Cor. 8:21). We are God's witnesses and, therefore, the opinion of us that others form is related to the opinion they have of Christ and His cause.

If you want to be a leader of God's people in whatever area, you will have a life of sacrifice over and above that of the typical sheep you pastor. If we cannot do this, if we are not willing to do this, if our wife or our family is not willing to do this, it would be better to say, "I did not know that this was the case; I think that it would be better for me not to take on such responsibility." There has never been a leader, secular or Christian, who has paid such a normal, ordinary price as that of everyone else. There has never been, and there never will be; for if such were the case, he would not be a leader.

The latest definition that we have continued to develop contains four fundamental aspects:

1. **God chooses and prepares the leader.** In John 15:16a, Jesus says, "You did not choose me, but I chose you." Moses was chosen by God just like every one of the prophets and apostles. God has always made this choice; He reserves this

right. He chooses His leaders because only He knows what He wants to do with them. God's choice is never without a defined purpose.

2. **The leader calls others to imitate his example.** We have already seen how Paul called his followers to imitate his example just as he sought to imitate Christ (1 Cor. 11:1). Leadership is more than teaching; it is modeling.

3. **There is a price to pay.** In Philippians 3:10, Paul allows us to see part of his desire: "My goal is to know him and the power of his resurrection and the fellowship of his sufferings, being conformed to his death." Our calling is twofold: 1) we were called to know Him and the power of His resurrection, and 2) we were called to participate in His suffering and become like Him in His death. Paul clearly understood that taking up his cross and following Christ means not only participating in His blessings, but taking place in His suffering, as well. There is a price to pay.

4. **The leader needs to pursue the goal that God has set.** On one occasion, Christ Himself said, "I can do nothing on my own. I judge only as I hear, and my judgment is just, because I do not seek my own will, but the will of him who sent me" (John 5:30). In this way, the Master, the second person of the Trinity, did not seek to establish goals, dreams, and purposes that were not according to the Father's will; much less can we, as human leaders, claim to lead others along any way that our finite mind can conceive.

Final Reflection

The spiritual leader must see himself as someone belonging to another category, but not a superior category. We belong to the community of the towel and basin. Perhaps the following illustration about Christ's way of thinking can help us:

> In my kingdom, on the other hand, a man becomes a great one, and a ruler, by being first the servant of those over whom he is to bear rule. In other states, they rule whose privilege it is to be ministered unto; in the divine commonwealth, they rule who account it a privilege to minister.[8]

Herein lies the difference. We do not have greater rights than those whom we lead just because we are leaders; we have greater responsibilities. What God has given us is not a superior appointment, but the privilege of being able to lead a people that He purchased with His blood; and this is an extraordinary privilege. Such is the case with the church. But in the case of the family, God gives children to parents so that they can seek to reproduce the image of Christ in those children. The husband receives the wife as a gift from God to lead her in the same way that Christ cares for and leads His church. Note Paul's instructions:

> Husbands, love your wives, just as Christ loved the church and gave himself for her to make her holy, cleansing her with the washing of water by the word. He did this to present the church to himself in splendor, without spot or wrinkle or anything like that, but holy and blameless. In the same way, husbands are to love their wives as their own bodies. He who loves his wife loves himself. (Eph. 5:25–28)

A spiritual leader should possess the following:

- A holy character
- An attitude of service
- A spirit of sacrifice
- A gentle spirit
- A love for God, His Word, and His people
- An authority subject to the Word
- A life dependent upon the Spirit of God and prayer
- A singular purpose: the glory of God
- A single measure of success: transformed lives
- One model alone: Jesus Christ[9]

CHAPTER 10

Be a Servant of Influence

*"[L]earn from me, because I am lowly
and humble in heart . . ."*
Matthew 11:29a

Introduction

The verse quoted above contains one of Jesus' most well-known phrases. Yet, at the same time, it is one of the teachings that we see least put into practice. With these words, the Master helped His disciples to understand that leadership in the kingdom of heaven is radically distinct to the model that they had known up until that point. Once again, we see how Christ is more interested in what we are than what we do. When He called His disciples, He told them that He would make them fishers of men; that is, they would become something beyond what they had been. Then, in Matthew 11:29a, He tells them, "[L]earn from me, because I am lowly and humble in heart." It is not enough to behave meekly and humbly. What is important to God goes beyond behavior.

When looking at redemptive history, we think that it would be easy to affirm the primary stumbling block for Christian leaders has been human pride. The greatest harm in the church of Christ can be traced back in one way or another to the heart of man. Falls may be diverse, but if we could establish a common denominator, we would have to conclude that the author of Proverbs certainly was correct when he said: "Pride comes before destruction, and an arrogant spirit before a fall" (Prov. 16:18). This was the case with Saul in the Old Testament and the case of Peter in the New Testament. We can see human pride on display in the following conversation between Jesus and Peter:

> Then Jesus said to them, "Tonight all of you will fall away because of me for it is written: 'I will strike the shepherd, and the sheep of the flock will be scattered.' But after I have risen, I will go ahead of you to Galilee."
>
> Peter told him, "Even if everyone falls away because of you, I will never fall away."
>
> "Truly I tell you," Jesus said to him, "tonight before the rooster crows, you will deny me three times."
>
> "Even if I have to die with you," Peter told him, "I will never deny you," and all the disciples said the same thing. (Matt 26:31–35)

Peter put more trust in his own words than in the words of Jesus Christ, who had just given him a warning. When Jesus announces to Peter that he would deny Him three times, instead of requesting help from God, he denied the truth of Christ's words by saying, "Even if I have to die with you, I will never deny you." What many people overlook is that the same human pride which confided in its own wisdom and knowledge was not just in Peter, but in the rest of the group. Take a look again at the words that follow Peter's statement: "[A]nd all the disciples said the same thing."

The pride found in human beings is what frequently prevents them from seeing their weaknesses and character flaws, even to the point of preventing them from seeking help before they experience a fall. Perhaps this spiritual blindness is the best explanation of why we often end up ruining the ministry that God gave us in the beginning.

Each leader needs to carry out his responsibilities from a position that enables him to influence others. Some do so from a position of humility; others, perhaps the majority, lead from a position of "being the boss," due to the pride that we have been analyzing. The prideful person enjoys being acknowledged as the boss, while the humble person leads by example, just like our Lord Jesus Christ.

We have already mentioned that the leader must model what he desires to see in his disciples, and this example must be perpetuated over time. If he does so only during the first few years, he will find that those who were with him initially were able to observe his walk; but because he did not continue living out his teachings, those who later join his ministry will have no idea what a true disciple actually is. The idea is for the leader to be able to continually and increasingly model the character of Christ and for his first disciples to be able to assimilate the way of leading in the kingdom of heaven so that those disciples who come later may imitate those who came before. Now, we can never forget that the leader who goes ahead continually needs to point to Christ because, *in the end, what we want to see are disciples who follow Christ and not us.* In other words, our followers need to see Jesus in us, and they need to understand that the only thing that we do is to follow in His footsteps. In his first letter, the apostle Peter reminds us of this principle when he writes: "For you were called to this, because Christ also suffered for you, leaving you an example, that you should follow in his steps" (1 Pet. 2:21).

All of this has to do with the leadership model of the kingdom of heaven. In the world, leaders frequently make use of
their power and authority, and, as such, their primary interest
is achieving the subjection and submission of those whom they
lead, instead of achieving the transformation of their character.
When Christ came, He purposed to model a lifestyle that would
transform the character of His disciples so that, over time, they
would look like Him. The power and authority that we alluded
to are intoxicating. When someone starts drinking alcohol, we
may note a certain happiness in his behavior, but as he drinks
more and more, spurred on by enjoyment, we will note how the
initial happiness frequently gives way to a state of foolishness
with consequences. This is regularly the case in the exercising of
power or authority. This is something that we can see throughout
the history of man, and it takes place because we don't realize
that power is corrupting us.

A good example in recent history is the life of Charles
Colson, who was the right hand of the American president,
Richard Nixon. When he rose to power along with Nixon,
Colson was thirty-nine years of age and was a graduate with honors from Brown University in the United States. He arrived at his
position with enormous integrity, to the point that he gave away
to others the Christmas gifts that had been given to him because,
as he himself said, no one was going to corrupt him. However,
later, he gave testimony of how during the reelection, he was
the mastermind of the famous Watergate scandal. A person so
upright ended up being corrupt and going to prison because he
thought, as he himself affirmed, that the continued presidency of
Nixon was necessary for the survival of the nation.[1] This was not
true at all, and was proven when Nixon resigned as president and
the nation moved on.

The only indispensable leader is Jesus, but this is how power
can deceive us. It gradually intoxicates us, persuades us, and
makes us think that we are indispensable. Jesus Christ, the head
of the Christian movement, died, and from that time on, we

see how the church became even stronger by the design of God Himself. The Lord knows what He is doing, and often when a leader dies, God shows in an even greater way how He truly is the only one who is irreplaceable. The Hebrew people entered the Promised Land and did so without "the great" Moses. They were guided by our GREAT GOD.

The Leader's Influence

The leader can occupy a position and get the people to do what he orders without necessarily achieving change of character in the people that he leads. This transformation of character should be the goal of every leader because it would be an important way of preparing people for when the leader passes away. It is noteworthy to see how Christ, above all other leaders in history, was able to prepare the leadership that would guide the effort, modeling a lifestyle that was consistent with His words. Christ's example was so influential that it was able to change the character of His followers. Position is often coveted, but we rarely see the holy character of an individual being coveted. One may desire someone else's character, but he is unlikely to covet it in the same way that he covets a position. When someone occupies a position, it often is the case that others covet it, but many times, God purposefully does not grant us position so that He first can work on the pride in us. Position only gives us the place needed for our meek and humble character to exercise influence. Position does not necessarily positively influence others' character, as we see in the lives of all of the emperors and dictators of the past. Christ, with a lower position than Pilate, was able to change a countless number of people.

One may arrive at a certain position due to favoritism, influence, or other non-biblical reasons such as manipulation of circumstances, which does not occur with character, which is something that must be cultivated. One can cultivate a holy or sinful character according to the example that he has chosen to follow. Chief executives, presidents of organizations, and even pastors frequently assume that the position they occupy is a sign of the character they possess, when in reality, these two things may be completely divorced from each other. One can have position and lack character or have an extraordinary character and lack position. Many use position to disguise their insecurities, as a way hiding their character flaws and making themselves feel better. This explains why many, when they lose their position, even lose their minds, because they lost the very thing that provided them security.

Christ never needed to occupy a position. In fact, He had position, but He did not feel the need to possess it because His sense of security was found in His relationship with God the Father. As such, He did not have to claim the position that was rather voluntarily given to Him by those who followed Him. We see this in the following words: "'Teacher,' they said, 'we know that you are truthful and teach truthfully the way of God. You don't care what anyone thinks nor do you show partiality'" (Matt. 22:16b). These words were pronounced by His opponents, which speaks to the fact that they came to recognize His authority. When the leader sees the need to claim his authority, this is an indication that, in reality, he does not possess it, and oftentimes others do not recognize it due to the weaknesses of character that he himself does not see even though others repeatedly have observed them. So, the best thing that he can do is to conceal them and let God do the rest. The reality is that it is not simply a matter of covering our faults, but of changing what is on the outside, which comes as a result of having changed what is on the inside.

The Influence of Pride and Humility

The vast majority of leaders who have been concerned about climbing the ladder of position have not spent the same amount of time and effort cultivating their character. Oftentimes, what motivates people to desire a position of importance is the existential void in which they live. Regrettably, once they arrive at the position of importance, they are still empty, which leads them to covet it more or to covet an even higher position. Likewise, this void may cause them to covet greater power within the position that they already have, or it may cause them to desire more people following them. If they do, in fact, think this way, the position will no longer be good enough for them, and they will develop new ambition.

Another reason for the hunger for position is insecurity. Position makes us feel above others and, as we lead, we make evident our sense of superiority to the point of wanting to demand that others recognize us as their superiors. *The reality is that, frequently, this type of leader is obeyed but not respected.* More often than not, people have more respect for someone who is in a lower position of leadership but possesses better character. The following is a good illustration of this: each one of us walks looking ahead of us and seeing others. If we could walk looking inward, perhaps we could better see our own faults. We need to stop and reflect or have someone help us by placing a mirror in front of us which allows us to see what we have not been able to observe before. Our best mirror is the Word of God, but man is capable of even seeing himself in that mirror and thinking that he is measuring up to God's standard. James puts it this way:

> But be doers of the word and not hearers only, deceiving yourselves. Because if anyone is a hearer of the word and not a doer, he is like someone looking at his own face in a mirror. For he looks at himself, goes away, and immediately forgets what kind of person he was. (James 1:22–24)

Finally, people covet climbing the ladder of position because of their hunger for power. This is a widespread sin because they want to control the other person and his circumstances in order to feel secure and to ensure that they get what they want. As this is this goal, people arrive at the conclusion that the way to accomplish this is by obtaining greater power. The reality is that we have never been in control. God is the ruler and general over His universe. The more it looks like we are in control, the more secure we think we are, but when we live like this, we will never feel completely secure. We affirm that God is in control, but we live assuming, at least subconsciously, that the only way to control is by having power over whatever it is that we want to control. We see this in the home where the wife seeks to control the husband and vice versa precisely because, when the husband thinks he has control over the wife, he feels more secure in the home. Ultimately, what we need is a solid relationship with God, which will allow us to live with the recognition that our sense of value and security is in Christ. Thus, we will not need all of these additional crutches, which also do not allow us to obtain what we are seeking. One way or another, all of us have made use of these crutches at some time in our life, or we even do so today. This is typical of human nature, and what we must do is to recognize it and work under God's direction.

The use of power in leadership was never the example of our Lord Jesus Christ. In fact, when He was given the opportunity to use power for His own benefit, He refused. In the garden of Gethsemane, we find one of these occasions:

> When those around him saw what was going to happen, they asked, "Lord, should we strike with the sword?" Then one of them struck the high priest's servant and cut off his right ear.
> But Jesus responded, "No more of this!" And touching his ear, he healed him. (Luke 22:49–51)

Peter's and Jesus' reaction to the same event were very different. Peter reacted in a fleshly way by cutting off the soldier's ear, and Christ reacted in a spiritual way and healed the wound. This is exactly what the leader must decide on every occasion: Do we react in order to glorify God, or do we react in order to carry out our own purpose? In the face of the same event, we can either hurt others or help them grow.

On one occasion, someone approached us before the Sunday service and told us that she wanted to leave the church. At that time, we did not know that this person had serious emotional problems. She said to us, "Pastors, I am leaving the church because no one likes me." We were aware that what she was saying was not true, because we knew of the different ways in which the church had helped her over the years. At that instant, we could have reacted to her with hurtful words for being "so ungrateful" to the church, or we could have acted in a way that would have helped her grow and move beyond the self-centeredness that was in her. So, we responded to her by saying, "We do not think that what you are saying is true, but if you feel this way, on behalf of the church, please forgive us." As soon as we uttered those words, she began to cry and said, "No. Forgive me. I am the problem. I know that I am." We consoled her and said, "Don't worry about it. We think that we have been able to show you evidence of our love." We said nothing more. We prayed, and the incident was over. We then began the worship service, and she never again made such an accusation. Words can soothe the soul, or they can be like acid to the skin. Often, what makes the difference is the degree of humility or pride within us.

Sadly, in these situations, the typical response is: "How could she say that after all that we have done for her and her family!" The truth is that for all of this individual's problems, this was the way that she viewed the love of others. This is wrong, but it was reality. So, we first told her the truth, indicating that we did not think she was correctly perceiving the church's love for her, but we later made her aware that if she felt that way (since, although distorted, this was her reality), on behalf of the church we asked her for forgiveness. Leaders must be greater than the offenses committed against them, and they should possess a heart that is forgiving of any hurt. We need to develop thick skin and a large heart.

The abuse of power is a "pagan" form of exercising leadership. Let us observe the following, which is an appropriate way of leading, according to the apostle Peter's instruction:

> I exhort the elders among you as a fellow elder
> and witness to the sufferings of Christ, as well as
> one who shares in the glory about to be revealed:
> Shepherd God's flock among you, not overseeing
> out of compulsion but willingly, as God would
> have you; not out of greed for money but eagerly;
> not lording it over those entrusted to you, but
> being examples to the flock. (1 Pet. 5:1–3)

Humble leaders who have been molded by God faithfully lead His people by being examples for the flock just as Jesus did during His time here on earth. But proud leaders look very different. Pride becomes angry when it is questioned because it sees every question as a threat. But God makes us grow. He transforms us into His image and sanctifies us, causing the typical characteristics of immaturity to disappear. Then, we look back and notice that whatever made us feel threatened and insecure was really insignificant and unimportant, although in the moment we saw it as threatening. In our insecurity, we often misinterpret the words and intentions of others when we feel like they are questioning us, but perhaps this was not their intent.

The Profile of a Proud Leader

The proud leader does not tolerate others leading alongside him because he perceives others as competition, which causes him to feel threatened again and again. This is why proud leaders tend to lead alone. They do not tolerate the slightest questioning from others, or they fear that others could leave them and set up shop somewhere else. The first time we started a training group

for future, potential leaders, someone made the following observation: "You have to be careful because you train them, and then
they leave you!" To which we responded: "If that happens, great!
Because they are going somewhere else and will have influence
in a place where perhaps we would never go. Praise the Lord!"
Perhaps God wishes to use us as a springboard to form some
other person to be impactful for the kingdom of heaven wherever God takes him in the future. Christ never felt threatened,
and, therefore, never said, "This must be done because I am the
Messiah," although He was. He also did not say, "This must be
done because I am the second person of the Trinity," and He is.
He did not have to tout His credentials.

Proud leaders want to be obeyed simply because of their
position. While it is true that part of our calling is to submit to
authority, it is no less true that such obedience should not be
blind. When we obey blindly, we can end up sinning by obeying
the leader but violating the Word of God. When obeying means
sinning against God, we must obey God before men (Acts 4:19).

Pride tends to use position, power, and even personality. A
charismatic and extroverted personality may be used sinfully to
benefit the leader's purposes. Now, perhaps charisma can buy
the leader people and followers, but it will not sustain him in the
moments of crisis. The character and convictions formed from
the Word of God are those things that will sustain the leader in
the midst of crisis. Regrettably, many people lack convictions.
We have ideas and opinions that we defend in conversations
and discussions, but convictions are what sustain us along the
way. Opinions are easy to change because we are the ones who
hold them, but we cannot do the same with our convictions.
Unfortunately, we live in the midst of a generation that is not
convinced of any truth and brings instability.

The proud leader wants to look good for others. Human
opinion is more important for him than God's opinion. He says
he believes one way, but he lives the other. In 1 Samuel 15, we
read about one of the examples of Saul's disobedience. The

Jewish king spared the life of Agag, king of the Amalekites, and the best animals, thus violating the Lord's order to completely and entirely destroy everything that breathed. When the prophet Samuel confronted Saul with his sin, these were a few of his words:

> Saul answered Samuel, "I have sinned. I have transgressed the LORD's command and your words. Because I was afraid of the people, I obeyed them." (v. 24)

> Saul said, "I have sinned. Please honor me now before the elders of my people and before Israel. Come back with me so I can bow in worship to the LORD your God." (v. 30)

Saul feared the people (v. 24) when he should have feared God. Also, he begged Samuel to honor him in the presence of the elders, the people, and the whole of Israel (v. 30). That is, he was interested in being honored in the presence of men, even after being rejected by God (v. 26). There is no better example than this to illustrate how the proud long for the approval of others. Saul behaved contrary to the voice of God because proud leaders rely on their own judgment to act.

The following is a good list of questions for self-evaluation that all who seek to be a servant with true spiritual influence should ask:

- Do you consider yourself superior to others?
- Do you want others to think that you have all the answers?
- Do you want others to consider you a humble person?
- Do you think that everyone else has a problem with ego?
- Is it difficult for you to ask for help?

- Do you try to control people or situations?
- Do you seek to carry out your will or God's will?
- Do you frequently think that you are right and everyone else is wrong?
- Are you offended when others criticize you?
- Is it difficult for you to ask for forgiveness?
- Is it difficult for you to submit to authority?[2]

The Profile of a Humble Leader

Humble leaders do not trust in their own wisdom or training, on their achievements or their gifts and abilities; rather, their trust is placed in God alone. The humble leader is one who has understood and applied the wisdom of the author of Proverbs who says, "Trust in the LORD with all your heart, and do not rely on your own understanding; in all your ways know him, and he will make your paths straight. Don't be wise in your own eyes; fear the LORD and turn away from evil" (Prov. 3:5–7).

Humility is the number one characteristic of people whom God uses; therefore, humble leaders may exercise greater influence than those who lack this quality. The proud person is usually selfish, but this is an egotistical attitude of the flesh that must be replaced by a humble attitude of the Spirit. This is the virtue that Jesus talked about when He said that we must learn directly from Him, as we saw this at the beginning of this chapter. The Lord commanded us to learn from Him, because as we live our lives learning from everyone but Him. We learn . . .

- from our selfish parents;
- from our worldly masters;
- from books that do not reflect the mind of God;
- from books filled with worldly values;
- from worldly friends;
- from the press; and

- from everyone except those from whom we
  should learn.

No selfish person can be humble. Humility is the result of having evaluated ourselves in the light of God's standard and of having seen our inner condition, which allows us to realize how small, needy, and dependent we are. Second, humility thinks first in the well-being of others, which is something that we do not do naturally. This is why the apostle Paul instructed the Philippians: "Do nothing out of selfish ambition or conceit, but in humility consider others as more important than yourselves. Everyone should look not to his own interests, but rather to the interests of others" (Phil 2:3–4).

Now, keep in mind that many people who think about the well-being of others are not humble. Firemen, physicians, nurses, etc., work for the good of others, but this does not necessarily make them humble. Note, once again, how humility is forged and manifested according to Philippians 2:3b: "but in humility consider others as more important than yourselves." We must regard others as more important than ourselves. But what does this mean? How do we consider others as more important than ourselves? We do so in the following ways:

- When we consider the likes, preferences, desires, interests, and points of view of others before considering our own.
- When making decisions, we think first of how they will affect our brother or sister and not how they will benefit our plans and ideas.
- When we are willing to sacrifice ourselves for the benefit of others, no matter what the cost.

This is exactly what Paul says in Philippians 2:4: "Everyone should look not to his own interests, but rather to the interests of others." Sadly, our fears and insecurities cause us to think of ourselves first as a survival mechanism, in the same way as a shipwrecked sailor, for fear of drowning, does not think of others around him.

The result of living this way is clearly expressed in verse 2: "[M]ake my joy complete by thinking the same way, having the same love, united in spirit, intent on one purpose."

Paul seems to be experiencing a certain degree of sadness concerning the disagreements that he has heard about his two partners in ministry: Euodia and Syntyche (Phil. 4:2). But beyond that, he seems to see what others do not: that divisions in the churches begin with two people who gradually gain followers. He knows that, if this conflict between these two sisters is not resolved, it will escalate to the point of potentially putting at risk the unity of the church at Philippi.

Allow me to show you how this occurs so that we may see how who we are influences others. In his book *The Joy of Living*, J. Dwight Pentecost tells us that on one occasion in a Dallas church, a conflict arose that grew to the point that two groups were formed and litigated against one another in order to see which of the two groups would retain control of the church property. Eventually, a decision favorable to one of the groups was handed down, and the other group ended up separating and starting another church. It was later reported in one of the Dallas newspapers that one of the elders of the church complained that at a church activity he had received a smaller piece of meat than a child sitting next to him.[3] This is how problems get started. In this case, one of the elders of the church was responsible for starting this controversy that ended up splitting a local church. Pride rises to the surface even in the most insignificant of acts.

The phrase "thinking the same way"(Phil. 2:2), which appears in the passage of Paul's letter to the Philippians, which we quoted earlier, comes from an expression that, in the original language, means to be of or have the same mind. If we have the mind of Christ in the revealed Word and think by means of the Holy Spirit who dwells within us, we should be able to agree on what it means to be of the same mind or thinking the same way.

This requires humility. Thinking the same way does not mean that we always have the same opinion, but it does mean that we can set aside our offensive weapons for the sake of unity as long as the truth of Christ is not being violated. We must be aware of the "monster" within us. William Barclay, in his commentary on the Letter to the Philippians, said, "The one danger which threatened the Philippian church was that of disunity. There is a sense in which this is the danger of every healthy church. It is when people are really in earnest and their beliefs really matter to them, that they are apt to get up against each other. The greater their enthusiasm, the greater the danger that they may butt heads. It is against that danger that Paul wishes to safeguard his friends."[4]

Thinking the same way . . .

- requires us to adjust and do things in accordance with what God has revealed;
- involves making every effort, in prayer and reflection, to gain an understanding of what is being discussed in light of God's revelation; and
- requires spiritual maturity.

Let us remember that humility is the backbone of all good leadership. Humble leaders cultivate relationships, train and mold others, invite others to lead along with them, share their ideas, and allow themselves to be questioned in a proper and constructive way.

Martin Lloyd-Jones said, "The man who is truly meek is amazed that God and man can think of him as well as they do and treat him as well as they do."[5]

Final Reflection

When it comes to training leaders, we cannot take this responsibility lightly; the process is as important as the final product (the goal). The speed at which leaders are formed perhaps explains the multitude of reports of shame and failure that we hear about both within and outside of the ministry. Christ took the time to train His disciples. We must not forget this. Character is not formed overnight; all things of quality require time and effort. A good example of this is the diamond because it is formed at great depths, under the highest of pressure, and over a long period of time. The same is true of character.

As leaders of today, we must continuously remember the value of integrity. Daily, we live the tension between what we want to do and what we should do. It is then that integrity of character determines the rules of the game in order to resolve such tension; it also determines what we will be, regardless of circumstances and people. If the leader's actions or intentions are in constant opposition, then one need only examine his character to understand what produces this dichotomy. Sadly, pride often leads us to compromise our integrity. Pride will always want to look good, although it must lie to do so. Pride leads man toward ungratefulness because he does not appreciate what others do and frequently believes himself to be worthy of what he has received. Perhaps the most common stumbling block of humans in general and of leaders in particular is pride and an inflated self-concept.

Humility is so valued that many are willing to overlook some of our weaknesses because they appreciate our humility. In the story of the Old Testament, there was likely no other leader greater than Moses, and of him God said, "Moses was a very humble man, more so than anyone on the face of the earth" (Num. 12:3). It was humility that God formed in Moses over the course of forty years in the desert while working for his father-in-law (at least for part of that time). Then, God continued to forge Moses for the next forty years as he led the Hebrew people to the Promised Land. Every great leader has first been a great follower.

Finally, let us keep in mind that after God's approval, the most important thing in the life of a leader is not the position that he occupies or the title he holds, but the integrity of character with which he lives, the consistency of his words and actions. The formation of character is something that cannot be taken lightly; we must dedicate ourselves to intentionally forming it. Talent is a gift, but character is a choice we make. May we not forget that our character is formed, either for good or bad, when we make decisions.

===== **CHAPTER II** =====

Be a Servant of Purpose

*For David, after serving God's purpose in his own generation,
fell asleep, was buried with his fathers, and decayed.*

Acts 13:36

Introduction

It is said that, years ago, the police found the famous German philosopher Schopenhauer sitting in the gutter of the street at about five o'clock in the morning. They approached him and asked, "Who are you?" They did not know who he was, and it seemed strange for them to come upon a man sitting in such a place at that time of the morning. The philosopher's response was, "I would love to know!" For Schopenhauer, life was nothing more than suffering, and even though man might be able to escape his sufferings for a moment, he will end up falling into a vacuum of boredom. According to him, human existence is a constant movement between pain and monotony or boredom.[1] This is what an intelligent life looks like, but without God.

Schopenhauer was a famous and intelligent philosopher who had dedicated time to considering the meaning of life, and years later, he did not know who he was. The pursuit of this great philosopher has turned out to be the question many teenagers ask when they do not know what the purpose of their lives is. There are people in their fifties and sixties who often express a sense of emptiness even after having lived over half of their life.

On one occasion, I had the opportunity to speak to an ex-general from our country, and I said to him, "General, you are in your eighties, and we know a little bit about your history. You made a name for yourself, had power, had money, and you have lived for many years . . . What do you feel at your age after having been who you were?" And with tears in his eyes, he said to me, "Doctor, I feel empty!" So, I asked him, "Do you know why you feel empty?" His answer was a denial. I asked him if he wanted to know why he felt empty. He nodded his head, and I proceeded to share the gospel with him. That day, this five-star general with money, name, power, and fame gave his life to the Lord and discovered what the great British journalist, author, thinker Malcom Muggeridge discovered in his own life. Pay attention to Muggeridge's words:

> I may, I suppose, regard myself, or pass for being, a relatively successful man. People occasionally stare at me in the streets: that's fame. I can fairly easily earn enough to qualify for admission to the higher slopes of the Internal Revenue: that's success. Furnished with money and a little fame even the elderly, if they care to, may partake of trendy diversions: that's pleasure. It might happen once in a while that something I said or wrote was sufficiently heeded for me to persuade myself that it represented a serious impact on our time: that's fulfillment. Yet I say to you—and I beg you to believe me—multiply these tiny triumphs by a million, add them all together, and

Pessy Lee - Is that all There is

they are nothing—less than nothing, a positive impediment—measured against one draught of that living water Christ offers to the spiritually thirsty, irrespective of who or what they are.[2]

This source of satisfaction that Muggeridge talks about is what Adam lost.

The Lost Man

There is a significant group of people who live seeking after success in order to find meaning and purpose in their life, but the motivators of success are all wrong:

- Unhappiness
- Insecurity
- Inferiority
- Anxiety
- Unsatisfaction
- Incompleteness

The primary driving force of humanity since the Fall of Adam is the search for meaning, purpose, or sense. We can see this reality in the pages of the book of Ecclesiastes. If there is anyone who clearly shows us man's search for purpose, his anxiety, and the acute pain and despair he experiences, it is the author of this book. Note his groans in the following verses taken from chapters 1 and 2 of Ecclesiastes:

> I, the Teacher, have been king over Israel in Jerusalem. I applied my mind to examine and explore through wisdom all that is done under heaven. God has given people this miserable task to keep them occupied. I have seen all things that are done under the sun and have found everything to be futile, a pursuit of the wind. (1:12–14)

I applied my mind to know wisdom and knowledge, madness and folly; I learned that this too is a pursuit of the wind. For with much wisdom is much sorrow; as knowledge increases, grief increases. (1:17–18)

Later on, we read:

I said to myself, "Go ahead, I will test you with pleasure; enjoy what is good." But it turned out to be futile. I said about laughter, "It is madness," and about pleasure, "What does this accomplish?" I explored with my mind the pull of wine on my body—my mind still guiding me with wisdom—and how to grasp folly, until I could see what is good for people to do under heaven during the few days of their lives.

I increased my achievements. I built houses and planted vineyards for myself. I made gardens and parks for myself and planted every kind of fruit tree in them. I constructed reservoirs for myself from which to irrigate a grove of flourishing trees. I acquired male and female servants and had slaves who were born in my house. I also owned livestock—large herds and flocks—more than all who were before me in Jerusalem. I also amassed silver and gold for myself, and the treasure of kings and provinces. I gathered male and female singers for myself, and many concubines, the delights of men. So I became great and surpassed all who were before me in Jerusalem; my wisdom also remained with me. All that my eyes desired, I did not deny them. I did not refuse myself any pleasure, for I took pleasure in all my struggles. This was my reward for all my struggles. When I considered all that I had

accomplished and what I
I found everything to be
the wind. There was noth
the sun. (2:1–11)

No one can describe the purs
in these verses.

The Origin of

God created Adam and Eve,
purpose, and they ruined it bef
note of the following life purpose

So God created man in
ated him in the image o
male and female.
God blessed them,
"Be fruitful, multiply, fil
it. Rule the fish of the s
and every creature that
(Gen. 1:27–28)

We have read and heard the
longer grab our attention. But t
purpose:

- Multiplying the human
filled with people who
of God. Populating the
image of God everywh
- Dominating and devel
point of exercising cont
air and the fish of the s
The full administration
creation here on earth.

ork after the Fall. This is the
book of Ecclesiastes, who also
icance in life. For the Preacher
his book gives himself), life was
plied all of the wisdom that he
derstand life, and he found it to be
enigmatic. Such an enigma that
his is how he expresses it:

o know wisdom and knowl-
folly; I learned that this too
wind. For with much wisdom
is knowledge increases, grief
1:17–18)

r thought that by cultivating wisdom he
life, as many philosophers throughout
ut in the end, he realized that wisdom
uch was Solomon's emphasis, putting his
ly seeking after and studying "all that is
Eccles. 1:13) that the words *wise* and *wisdom*
es throughout the book of Ecclesiastes, and
eventeen appear in the section cited earlier.
siastes found himself frustrated because even
had not helped him solve the great enigma
been able to (nor can we) change things. This
n: "What has been is what will be, and what
what will be done" (Eccles. 1:9a). And later he
rooked cannot be straightened; what is lacking
ted" (Eccles. 1:15). When man fails to move the
his own way, he turns on himself; he becomes
ind, therefore, incapable of seeing life how God
sees it. Everything then begins to be interpreted through his
person, and the best biblical evidence of this is provided by
the author of Ecclesiastes. There has never existed a more self-
centered man than Solomon at his worst. Hence his need to have

had labored to achieve,
... and a pursuit of

there was no true Love in Solomon or for Solomon

some thousand women. First Kings 11:3 mentions that he had seven hundred wives who were princesses and three hundred concubines. In the book of Ecclesiastes, only the concubines are mentioned. "The Hebrew word here for 'concubines' (*šiddāh*) is related to the word *shad*, which means 'breast.' This is why some translators translate 'concubines' as 'breasts' and 'many concubines' as 'abundant breasts.'"[3] It is a "crude reference to women who are used for sexual pleasure only."[4]

If you want to know how self-centered a man can become who has turned away from God and has no purpose in life, then take a close look at the following phrases recorded in the first eleven verses of Ecclesiastes 2:

1. I said to myself (v. 1)
2. I explored with my mind (v. 3)
3. on my body (v. 3)
4. my mind still guiding me (for the second time in v. 3)
5. I increased my achievements (v. 4)
6. I built and planted (v. 4)
7. I made and planted (v. 5)
8. I constructed (v. 6)
9. All who were before me (v. 7)
10. I also amassed silver and gold (v. 8)
11. I gathered male and female singers for myself (v. 8)
12. I became great (v. 9)
13. All that my eyes desired (v. 10)
14. I did not refuse myself any pleasure (v. 10)
15. I took pleasure in all my struggles (v. 10)
16. This was my reward for all my struggles (v. 10)
17. When I considered all that I had accomplished (v. 11)
18. I had labored to achieve (v. 11)

As we can see, the author of this book refers to himself a multitude of times. This is how the man without purpose, direction, and meaning lives. Regrettably, what this man and any other self-centered man does not understand is that no one can feel satisfied centered on himself. It has never been possible, nor will it ever be. As someone once said, "When a man is wrapped up in himself, he makes a pretty small package."[5]

The author of Ecclesiastes was unable to find the solution to the enigma of life because his search focused on . . .

- his own observation;
- his own reasoning;
- his own experience; and
- his own conscience.

It seems to have never occurred to him that the Creator of life is the only one who has the answer to the mystery or profound questions of life. This man experienced all areas of the human endeavor and never found purpose or meaning. This is why he concluded that seeking pleasure in life is like chasing after the wind. Try to trap the wind, and you will see how it simply slips through your fingers. In the same way, for Solomon, trying to understand the meaning of life was foolishness because it would immediately slip from his mind. His advice for us would be that we try not to do so; he already tried, and it produced no result.

What we discover throughout the book of Ecclesiastes is not only a void, but an emotional pain as a fruit of not being able to find a reason for living. There is no doubt that the wine the author of Ecclesiastes talks about, the sexual promiscuity that he experienced, the multiple construction projects he participated in, the many gardens that he planted, and the numerous vineyards that he cultivated were nothing more than his attempt to anesthetize the pain with which he could not live. The author of this book must have experienced a deep sense of depression.

This state of being is so common today that many refer to it as the age of melancholy, unlike the age of anxiety as was called the age immediately after the Second World War.[6] After this war, the production capability of the United States was greater than what the people were purchasing and, therefore, it was thought necessary to convince the people to consume more as a way of stimulating the economy. Precisely around this time, marketing techniques began to proliferate. In 1950, Vance Packard wrote a book entitled *The Hidden Persuaders* in which he describes how to channel unconscious behaviors and how to manipulate purchasing habits.[7] Since then, consumerism has been the dominant economic theory in the northern hemisphere, but at the same time, we would say that it is the number one life philosophy of the population. It is the primary anesthetic for the existential pain of the majority of the population. Hence the proliferation of shopping malls, which could be catalogued as the preferred house of worship in our day. The god who is worshiped is "me," and the religion through which "me" is worshiped is hedonism. The hedonist's problem is that he seeks pleasure that can only be found in God. The psalmist says it this way: [I]n your presence is abundant joy; at your right hand are eternal pleasures" (Ps. 16:11). The first part of this verse says: "You reveal the path of life to me . . ." The path of life takes us to the presence of God, and there we find all joy, all pleasure, and all delight that the hedonist seeks. The hedonist desires these pleasures for his flesh and not for his soul. When he experiences pleasure in the flesh, his soul continues to be unsatisfied. Instead of understanding that his dissatisfaction comes from a much deeper void, he understands that it comes from the desire for more pleasures of the flesh. And for him, one thousand women like those that Solomon came to possess are not enough to satisfy this human void.

The Solution

Since the Fall, man has worshiped false gods in search of what he is missing. And everything that he has undertaken has been yet another cistern that provides water to satisfy his thirst, but only for a moment because it is a cracked cistern incapable of holding water (see Jer. 2:13). Only Christ has the water that can satisfy man for eternity. If the human is to find purpose in life, he first will have to understand that we were created to know God and to have a relationship with Him. This is a great privilege; therefore, in Jeremiah 9:23–24a, God reveals how we should live:

> The wise person should not boast in his wisdom; the strong should not boast in his strength; the wealthy should not boast in his wealth. But the one who boasts should boast in this: that he understands me and knows me.

Life is an opportunity that God has given us to know Him personally and intimately as we pursue His glory; and when we pursue His glory, we find joy.

All that the human does should flow out of his relationship with God. If there is anything that men, unlike women, frequently do not have, it is a good relationship with their Creator. God made us to have dominion over the earth but under his lordship. Nevertheless, after the Fall of Adam and Eve, man has sought his sense of meaning and purpose in what he does and not in Christ. If what he does is what primarily brings him satisfaction, we have to ask: What will happen when he can no longer do what he is doing now? He will lack purpose in life. How will he feel when others do things better than he does? Jealous? Envious? What will happen when he no longer feels in control of what he does? He will feel insecure and return to being a perfectionist and perhaps neurotic.

Much of human fear, jealousy, and envy is nothing more than the result of living comparing ourselves to others instead of finding our sense of identity in Christ as our model. Work within the fallen conditions of the planet will never be able to satisfy the needs of fallen man. When God gave man the responsibility of working, it was supposed to be part of his purpose in life. But Adam should have done his work for God's glory and under His

CHAPTER 13

Be a Reflexive Servant

No one considers, nor is there
knowledge or discernment . . .
Isaiah 44:19a ESV

Introduction

"Superficiality is the curse of this age. The doctrine of instant satisfaction is a primary spiritual problem. The desperate need today is not for a greater number of intelligent people, or gifted people, but for deep people."[1] This description that author and pastor Richard Foster makes of our time is what encouraged me to include an invitation to reflection here toward the end of this book.

The accelerated pace of life with which modern man lives is his first obstacle to reflection. One of our greatest frustrations consists of the dichotomy that we frequently see between the Christian's attitude while listening to the Sunday sermon and saying "amen," and the way he lives during the rest of the week.

Such a divorce of behavior may have several causes, but in our opinion, one of them is that the sermon people hear on Sunday morning has a very ephemeral life, as it typically lasts between forty-five minutes to an hour at most; but after they leave church, the large majority of believers do not go back and meditate on the things that they just heard. It is impossible for such a short exposure to contribute to significant change in the believer's mindset, much less the unbeliever's. When it comes to reading a book, something similar occurs. We read several pages at a time, and if we do not go back and meditate on the most important things, what we read escapes our mind. "Books don't change people, paragraphs do—sometimes sentences."[2] These are the words of John Piper with which we so deeply identify and, because so, we have dedicated this chapter to reflecting upon phrases that in one way or another have contributed to changing important aspects of our life while being highly practical at the same time. Regarding some of these phrases, we remember perfectly well who said them or where we read them, but in other cases we do not know from where they originated. Some of the phrases that appear in this section are the result of our own reflection. In a way, this last part of the book can be a sort of testimony of how God has used the phrases of some of His children to transform our thinking; and as the Word says so well, as a man thinks in his heart, so is he (see Prov. 23:7 NASB).

This book would be lacking if we did not include this chapter as part of its content. And we mention this because we live in the midst of a generation which is pragmatic, utilitarian, therapeutic, relativistic, situational, minimalistic, disconnected, emotional, and therefore, the enemy of sober and profound thought. People in our time do not like to think because it requires hard work. They want rapid and self-serving results. For those who are less familiar with these terms, we will take this opportunity to define them.

- **Pragmatic:** judging actions as good and valid based on results

- **Utilitarian:** judging the value of something based on the usefulness it represents
- **Therapeutic:** seeing sin as a sickness; therefore, therapy is what the individual needs and not repentance
- **Relativistic and Situational:** people and their circumstances determining what is moral
- **Minimalistic:** reducing everything to its minimum expression, including what is sacred
- **Disconnected:** not knowing what is occurring within and outside of oneself
- **Emotional:** making decisions based on emotions and not reason

All of this prevents the individual of our time from thinking seriously about his life and the society around him. If we are aware of the circumstances in which we find ourselves, we are able to understand the reasons perfectly well in light of what we have just stated.

Following are some ideas, phrases from others, and phrases of our own that have served us to refine our thinking and organize our lives.

Be a Biblical Person: *Three Questions for Evaluation*

During my first few years in the Christian faith, when I began to read literature to feed my soul, I found in one of the many books I read, whose title I do not remember, three questions which should be present in our minds when it comes time to make a decision or simply conduct our day-to-day lives. They are:

- Is this biblical?
- What is my motivation?
- Who will receive the glory?

These three questions are relatively simple, but they have the potential of causing a profound impact in the way we think and live. As a physician, I could ask myself if the way I practice medicine is biblical; I could ask if my motivation is earning money or serving others; and finally, I could ask myself who will receive the glory? Similarly, we could ask ourselves the same three questions regarding each sermon we have preached or regarding our married life.

The philosopher Protagoras wrongly stated: "Man is the measure of all things." In contrast, the author of Proverbs reminds us that there are ways which appear wise to man, but in the end, they lead to death (see Prov. 14:12). Therefore, we must continuously ask ourselves if our way of working or living is biblical. What we pursue is as important to God as the motivation behind it. The motivation for why we do something in particular has to do with the condition of our heart and the orientation of our life: vertical or horizontal. Sometimes we do not want to do something because we think that it does not measure up to who we are, or we do not want to do it because we feel that we should have been asked before anyone else. But when these thoughts arise, these three questions could help us evaluate our attitude.

Be a Person of Definite Purpose:
People Are the Purpose; His Glory Is the Goal

We often are so focused on doing things well (and we should do them well) that we forget that we do what we do not just to do it, but in order to serve others. In other words, we can live merely to do things, or we can live to serve others. Notice the posture of Christ in the following passage:

> The apostles gathered around Jesus and reported to him all that they had done and taught. He said to them, "Come away by yourselves to a remote place and rest for a while." For many people were

coming and going, and they did not even have time to eat.

So they went away in the boat by themselves to a remote place, but many saw them leaving and recognized them, and they ran on foot from all the towns and arrived ahead of them.

When he went ashore, he saw a large crowd and had compassion on them, because they were like sheep without a shepherd. Then he began to teach them many things.

When it grew late, his disciples approached him and said, "This place is deserted, and it is already late. Send them away so that they can go into the surrounding countryside and villages to buy themselves something to eat."

"You give them something to eat," he responded.

They said to him, "Should we go and buy two hundred denarii worth of bread and give them something to eat?"

He asked them, "How many loaves do you have? Go and see."

When they found out they said, "Five, and two fish." Then he instructed them to have all the people sit down in groups on the green grass. So they sat down in groups of hundreds and fifties. He took the five loaves and the two fish, and looking up to heaven, he blessed and broke the loaves. He kept giving them to his disciples to set before the people. He also divided the two fish among them all. Everyone ate and was satisfied. They picked up twelve baskets full of pieces of bread and fish. Now those who had eaten the loaves were five thousand men. (Mark 6:30–44)

Notice how the disciples had withdrawn to rest, as they did not even have time to eat. But as soon as Jesus saw the multitude, He had compassion on them. The disciples were given to the task: "Send them away so that they can go into the surrounding countryside and villages to buy themselves something to eat" (v. 36). But Jesus "had compassion on them, because they were like sheep without a shepherd" (v. 34). The way we live and work marks the difference. In church, beginning and ending the Sunday service is not what is most important, although it certainly is. The most important thing is if God has spoken to His people by His Word the message that He wanted them to hear that day. Did we honor God? Did we minister to the congregation? Did we preach His Word? The answers to these three questions are more important than anything else.

Be a Servant of His Will:
The Need Does Not Constitute the Call of God

We will continually have more demands than we can meet, and this can become a source of frustration. However, we must remember that we are only responsible for doing what God has called us to do. When Jesus went down to the pool of Bethesda, He did not heal every disabled person there. The text says that there were hundreds of disabled people, but He only healed one (John 5:1–9). Jesus could have multiplied the loaves every day in order to feed the hungry, but the Gospels register only two occasions when He did so. He understood perfectly well that He had come to do the will of His Father (John 6:38) and not His own nor that of anyone else. At the end of His days, Jesus did not say, "Father, thank You that I have healed all the sick." Nor did He say, "Father, thank You that I fed the hungry." Rather, these were His words: "I have glorified you on earth by completing the work you gave me to do" (John 17:4). No more and no less. On another occasion, Jesus declared: "I was sent only to the lost sheep of the house of Israel" (Matt. 15:24). He understood His mission. Others would come later with the mission of evangelizing unto the uttermost parts of the world, but Jesus knew what He had come to do. Likewise, at another time, Christ stated: "My hour has not yet come" (John 2:4b). If we are not careful, we will undertake a number of tasks that God never called us to do.

Be a Person of Excellence: *Excellence Honors God*

Ted Engstrom, former director of Youth for Christ and World Vision International, said that "the Christian leader never equates mediocrity with the things of God but is always committed to the pursuit of excellence."[3] We don't seek to do things with excellence so that others will applaud us; we should seek to do so because everything that is outside the realm of excellence does not reflect God's character. Now, excellence is not doing things better than others; excellence is doing what you can do in the best way possible. This is excellence. We may not preach the way that someone like Charles Spurgeon preached, but that should not be our measuring stick. The measure of our excellence is based on whether or not when we stand in the pulpit we can be confident before God that we have made our best effort of preparing, that we have given our best time of dedication, that we have managed to search the Scriptures, and that we have sought to deliver what God gave us in the best way possible. This is the excellence that we are discussing.

Sloppiness is not excellence. Putting off until tomorrow what can be done today is not excellence. Doing what we should do, when we should do it, and in the best way possible is excellence. Excellence has a price that must be paid all the time. A former president of the United States said, "There is no victory at bargain basement prices."[4]

Mediocrity denies God's character. Jesus said, "My Father is glorified by this: that you produce much fruit and prove to be my disciples" (John 15:8). He did not say that the Father was pleased with our bearing fruit, but much fruit. Our God is a God of abundance and excellence. The prophet Daniel distinguished himself by having an extraordinary spirit: he was a man of diligence, faithfulness, and integrity. This forms part of excellence. Let us not forget that if something deserves to be done, it deserves to be done with excellence. One of the criticisms that we most frequently have heard from the unbelieving world is the lack of excellence found in the Sunday services of many evangelical churches. We need only to see the beauty and wonder of God's creation to know how our Father desires us to reflect it.

Be a True Servant:
"The Measure of a Man Is Not How Many Servants He Has, But How Many Men He Serves"[5]

There is a story about a large group of European pastors that arrived at one of the Northfield Bible Conferences organized by D. L. Moody in Massachusetts at the end of the nineteenth century. Following the European custom of the time, each guest placed his shoes out for the hall staff to clean them during the night. However, there was no one to clean them because that was not the American custom.

As he walked through the dormitories that night, Moody saw the shoes and decided not to embarrass his brothers. He mentioned the need to some of the ministerial students, but no one was willing to help. Moody collected all of the shoes and, alone in his room, began to clean and polish the shoes. A friend stopped by Moody's room and saw him, but Moody said nothing.

When the European guests opened their doors the following morning, the shoes were clean. Moody never said anything, but his friend told a few people. So, during the rest of the conference, different men offered to shine the shoes in secret. This is a great example of what a true servant is and how he can influence others by his example.[6]

We must see ourselves as servants who serve others. Service is not simply a task, but a great privilege. A privilege is something that you care for, something you value, something you understand you do not deserve, but something that God has graciously granted you. Privileges are treated with holiness, care, diligence, and integrity. If we are going to serve, we must pray for our service, for the task we complete. For a long time, this was our prayer: "Lord, make me a minister of Your grace." It does not matter where we serve; we should be ministers of His grace: when we preach, when we teach, when we pray, when we speak, when we listen, in our friendships, etc. Finally, if we cannot be ministers of His grace, we are not ready to serve for God's glory. God desires instruments, prepared vessels, so that His grace can flow through those vessels. Things go well when the grace of God flows. The only thing that stops God's work, so to speak, is an obstacle that prevents the natural flow of His grace. He naturally makes His character flow through His instruments.

Be a Just Person:
"There Is Nothing More Unequal Than the Equal Treatment of Unequal People"

When I was just twelve years old, I read this phrase in a book owned by my father called *The Education of the Exceptional Child*. Our father had died, and we were looking through some of the documents that he had left in a few drawers. We found this book in one of those drawers. For some reason, this phrase stuck in my mind and has remained there to this day. When it comes time to serve, we must remember that God's standard never changes, but the application of His standard requires wisdom. We would not ask a one-year-old child to use the restroom without our help, although we would require a ten-year-old to do so. If, as a pastor, we sin after more than thirty years in the Christian faith, God will judge us differently than someone who was converted just last night. James, one of the authors of the

New Testament, reminds us of this truth in another way: "Not many should become teachers, my brothers, because you know that we will receive a stricter judgment" (James 3:1). In the same congregation there are people in different stages of sanctification. Therefore, our level of patience must be higher for those who have been in the family of God for much less time. We must be just when it comes time to judge.

Be a Worshiper of the One True God: "We Become What We Worship"

G. K. Beale wrote a book titled *We Become What We Worship*, which includes a truth revealed in the book of Psalms:

> Their idols are silver and gold, made by human hands. They have mouths but cannot speak, eyes, but cannot see. They have ears but cannot hear, noses, but cannot smell. They have hands but cannot feel, feet, but cannot walk. They cannot make a sound with their throats. Those who make them are just like them, as are all who trust in them. (Ps. 115:4–8)

The prophet Jeremiah revealed that what the psalmist warned of became a reality among the Jews: "Declare this in the house of Jacob; proclaim it in Judah, saying: Hear this, you foolish and senseless people. They have eyes, but they don't see. They have ears, but they don't hear" (Jer. 5:20–21). Ezekiel condemned the same condition found among the people (Ezek. 12:1–2).

Think about who you are for a moment. What we are today is a reflection of what we have worshiped all throughout our lives. If you look at the apostle Paul and how he lived, you will realize that he was a reflection of what he worshiped. Likewise, we have many idols in our hearts, and those idols shape us. The following questions may help us to find some of our idols:

- Are we willing to sin in order to follow it?
- Are we willing to sin if we think we will lose it?
- Is this something that gives us value or importance?
- Will we become irritated as soon as someone speaks negatively about this person or thing?
- Is this something we need in order to feel safe?
- Are we willing to sacrifice relationships so that we do not lose it or defend it?

Our idols represent part of the human effort to live independently, trusting in people or things instead of trusting in God. "Sin is . . . the unwillingness of man to acknowledge his creatureliness and dependence upon God and his effort to make his own life independent and secure."[7] Our heart does not tolerate someone tampering with our idols. If this is the case, we need to renounce such idols. If we do not destroy our idols, they will end up destroying us.

Be a Productive Person: " *Right Now Counts Forever"*

I had just started taking my first few steps in the Christian faith when I heard this phrase by R. C. Sproul: "Right now counts forever." Latin culture, the culture I come from, is not characterized by living with a sense of urgency. There is a saying that goes like this: "Don't put off until tomorrow what you can do today." Sometimes we have jokingly said that it seems that some people have changed the saying to: "Don't do today what you can put off until tomorrow." When we live like this, our lives become complicated. As someone very well put it, a difficult job is nothing more than the accumulation of many small tasks that were not done on time or in the right way. We need a greater sense of urgency because we do not have all eternity on this side of glory to carry out the task that God has given us. When today is over, we will never see it again.

The apostle Paul instructed the Ephesians by telling them: "Pay careful attention, then, to how you walk—not as unwise people but as wise—making the most of the time, because the days are evil" (Eph. 5:15–16). When we wake up each morning, we should think about how God would want us to carry out His will that day. We cannot continue living in an irreflexive way because we will waste so much time and, along with it, we will lose many rewards when we arrive in the kingdom of heaven. Obviously, we do not work to accumulate rewards, but for God's glory. In the parable of the talents, the one who had received five talents turned them into ten, and the one who had received two talents turned them into four. However, the one who received one talent, kept it and returned it. The master praised the attitude of the first two servants and gave orders to remove the talent from the hand of the one who did not use his time to invest said talent. Thus, Christ illustrates what will happen when it comes time to give an account with those who have not used their opportunities and privileges that God has given them to glorify His name here on earth and contribute to the expansion of His kingdom.

This other phrase, attributed to Jim Elliott, sums up very well the intensity with which we should live: "Wherever you are, be all there! Live to the hilt every situation you believe to be the will of God." When my wife and I moved to the United States, where she is from originally, we did not live there for fifteen years longing for what we had left behind, because we understood that it would take away our concentration, effort, and dedication to God's will for us in that nation. Now, more than fifteen years have passed since we returned to the Dominican Republic, my country of origin, and we also do not long for all of the things we left behind there for the same reasons that we just mentioned. During His time on earth, Christ gave everything to complete the task given to Him by His Father, and this was His delight. At the end, He set out again to enjoy the love of the Father and the glory of God that He had enjoyed from eternity past.

Be a Wise Servant:
"Ideas Have Consequences"

This is a well-known saying in our day. In the midst of a generation that has created a moral revolution and sought to eliminate all value from those truths that have sustained humanity for hundreds and thousands of years, we must always remember that new ideas will have consequences for many years. G. K. Chesterton was entirely correct when he said, "Whenever you remove any fence, always pause long enough to ask yourself, 'Why was it put there in the first place?'" This is also the idea behind Proverbs 22:28, and they are wise words. If a retaining wall is built to contain a growing river, and the river ends up not growing after many years, a generation that is unaware of the floods of the past may come along and, having never seen one, decide to remove the wall, which would prove to be a fatal decision if the river were to grow again. God and the accumulated wisdom of men have left retaining walls against the wickedness of man. Beware! Our generation seems to be removing all the retaining walls that prior generations built. Our generation has removed the sense of duty, guilt, and shame from our midst; and now are beginning to reap the bad fruits of the first harvest.

In the case of the church of Christ, we have some twenty centuries of history, and therefore, we need to know the collective wisdom of the past from those men whom God gave to His church as teachers to navigate these turbulent times. Nothing is as simple as it appears. After Genesis 3, everything became complicated. Occasionally, someone stops us to ask us a question, saying, "Pastor, this will only take a minute," and he goes on to ask his questions. I will frequently respond with: "Do you want me to respond to that before Genesis 3 or after Genesis 3?" Because before Genesis 3, the question was very easy; after

Genesis 3 is another story, precisely because of the sinfulness of the human heart and mind.

Be a Person Who Is Prudent When Speaking:
Silence Is Usually Your Best Defense

Often the more you need to justify something, the less reason you have to defend it. James, in the New Testament letter which bears his name, warns us and advises us that "Everyone should be quick to listen, slow to speak, and slow to anger" (James 1:19b). We are prone to give an opinion without knowing all the facts and speak without knowing how we have sinned by contributing to what is occurring. The wise man knows when to speak and when to remain silent. The humble person knows that he does not need to defend himself in the large majority of cases. Both God and his own testimony represent his best defense. If God and his own testimony cannot defend him, nothing that he says will ever be able to. During the unjust trials carried out against Jesus, the Son of God remained silent during most of the interrogations or responded with only a few words. He knows better than anyone else the wisdom behind the book of Proverbs: "Don't answer a fool according to his foolishness or you'll be like him yourself. Answer a fool according to his foolishness or he'll become wise in his own eyes" (26:4–5).

There is a time to speak and a time to remain silent. Our defenses occasionally irritate others a lot and lead us to sin even more. Sometimes, in the midst of confusion, we lie in defense or twist the truth intentionally or subconsciously. Other times, we are the ones who get irritated in the middle of defending ourselves, and when this happens, we lose all objectivity. The wise and prudent man is not interested in winning, but in winning others by making use of grace and truth . . . in that order. Humility is not defensive; pride is. Love is not argumentative; self-centeredness is.

Be a Person of Prayer:
"Prayer Is Not Measured by How Much We Get from God, but by How Much of God Gets into Us"

This is one of many phrases by E. M. Bounds, a man very well-known for his prayer life. We are all convinced of the great necessity that we must pray continuously, and at the same time, the majority of God's children are dissatisfied with their prayer life. In our view, everything begins with a misunderstanding of the purpose of prayer. The majority of believers measure the effectiveness of their prayers by the number of positive responses that they receive from God. When God responds with "no," or when He says, "not yet," or when He says, "my grace is sufficient," the believer considers all of these responses to be unanswered prayers. When we say that God is immutable and that no one can change His will, we almost immediately hear the other person say, "Well, why do we pray?" We must always remember that prayer was not designed to change God's will, but to enter into His purposes.

When Jesus taught His disciples to pray, one of the things He taught them to pray for was that the will of God would be done "on earth as it is in heaven" (Matt. 6:10). And when Jesus found Himself in the midst of His most difficult hour in the garden of Gethsemane, these were His words: "My Father, if it is possible, let this cup pass from me. Yet not as I will, but as you will" (Matt. 26:39b). The second person of the Trinity, with all rights and privileges, with all wisdom possible, did not pray to change the Father's will. Changing God's will to make way for our own will is to move from the sacred to the carnal, from the perfect to the imperfect, and from wisdom to human folly. In prayer, God prepares our heart and mind for the circumstances that come up along the way. It is in intimacy that God reminds us of His truth, His love for us, and His faithfulness to His own. Also, it is in intimacy that our strength is renewed. We need to pray before we do. We can do nothing without praying; but we can do anything (hyperbolically speaking) after praying. Jesus said it in a different way: "you can do nothing without me" (John 15:5).

Be a Servant Who Understands Pain:
"It Is Doubtful Whether God Can Bless a Man Greatly Until He Has Hurt Him Deeply"

Those who are familiar with A. W. Tozer may know this quote, which is found in his book *The Root of the Righteous*, in the chapter titled "Praise God for the Furnace."[8] This was a man who understood from the biblical record that God uses the pain of suffering to break our guilt and destroy the walls that we have built around our heart which are preventing the formation of the character of Christ in us. This was the case in the life of Joseph, Moses, Job, Jeremiah, Peter, Paul, and many others, some of whom appear in chapter 11 of Hebrews. Also, as God revealed to the apostle Paul, God perfects His power in weakness (2 Cor. 12:9). In other words, nothing allows the display of God's power and glory like man's weakness. The best example of this is the Lord Jesus Christ Himself hanging on a cross after having been beaten and mocked. Only God understands what He is doing because His wisdom is inscrutable. But a true servant of God needs to trust in the goodness of his Lord, in His sovereignty, in His providence, and in His work. Many times, man makes his spiritual and emotional situation worse by questioning the character of God in the midst of the trial. This does not bring us peace, and it greatly increases our pain.

The psalmist, with less revelation than we have today because most of the Bible had not yet been written, understood that God has good purposes for His children in the midst of difficulties. This is why he wrote in Psalm 119: "It was good for me to be afflicted so that I could learn your statutes" (v. 71). With these words, the author of this psalm helps us to understand that we often do not learn the statutes of our God until we have been broken because, up until that point, in our foolishness, we insist on doing things our way; thus, we hinder the purposes of God, at least temporarily, as was the case with Jonah. Later, the psalmist speaks of how he was able to make it through the difficulty of the moment and says: "If your instruction had not been my delight, I would have died in my affliction" (v. 92). If the psalmist had become angry at God, as many do, he would have been consumed in self-pity, which is a pessimistic and self-centered feeling where the person sees himself as the biggest victim of all that has occurred or is occurring around him. Joseph, even after his brothers had sold him, did not feel this way because he knew that God was not unconcerned with his experience; therefore, when his brothers found themselves in his presence years later, they did not find a resentful Joseph, as we see in the following words: "You planned evil against me; God planned it for good to bring about the present result—the survival of many people" (Gen. 50:20).

Final Reflection

If you want to "be before you do," you need to cultivate your mind, so that you do not waste it. Now, remember that your mind is not your brain. The brain is an organ, while the mind is an ability given to man by God, which uses cerebral capabilities, but at the same time makes use of the conscience and the image of God in man to reason ideas that sooner or later will have consequences. God called us to love Him with all our heart, soul, and mind (Matt. 22:37), as we have already seen. He also called us to be transformed by the renewing of our mind (Rom. 12:2). He knows the importance of how man thinks because every action is preceded by a thought. We sin in thought long before we sin in action. This is why Jesus said that "everyone who looks at a woman lustfully has already committed adultery with her in his heart" (Matt. 5:28).

Not cultivating our mind is wasting or making poor use of one of the greatest gifts that God has ever given to man. Animals do not have such capability nor does any other being on earth. It is something that forms part of the image of God in man. Therefore, if such is true, how could we not make our greatest effort to feed our mind with the wisdom of God?

Another way of renewing and transforming our mind is by continually analyzing the events of life through the lens of the Bible. Reading Christian literature written by individuals who have been gifted by God with wisdom and discernment contributes to making us even wiser. And in this sense, I would like to emphasize that we have a legacy of two thousand years of history during which thousands of servants of God have recorded for posterity what they have learned about our God. Not making use of this legacy is neither humble nor wise.

CHAPTER 14

Be a Servant Who Is Not Seduced by Success

"Above all, be strong and very courageous to observe carefully the whole instruction my servant Moses commanded you. Do not turn from it to the right or the left, so that you will have success wherever you go. This book of instruction must not depart from your mouth; you are to meditate on it day and night so that you may carefully observe everything written in it. For then you will prosper and succeed in whatever you do."

Joshua 1:7–8

Introduction

Without a doubt, prosperity and success have caused many people to succumb to adversity. "For one man who can stand prosperity, there are a hundred that will stand adversity."[1] Prosperity tends to make man proud, self-sufficient, indifferent to others, and insensitive to the precariousness of others. Adversity, on the other hand, frequently brings man closer to God. Society has always been in search of security and fame;

these two conditions by themselves make man seek after success and prosperity. It is unfortunate that the same sinful thirst of man has infiltrated the church of our time and, as a consequence, has given birth to an entire movement, conceived in hell itself, known as the prosperity gospel. This movement originated in Hades and leads people to its place of origin. We say this without fear of being wrong because it is a movement which has distorted the gospel and has made money and riches the number one pursuit of man. Moreover, this movement teaches that sickness does not form part of God's will for any of His children. It has often made the gospel a message of riches, health, and happiness that could well represent the measure of success for many people. Let us pay attention to the testimony of Malcom Muggeridge at seventy-five years of age:

> Indeed, I can say with complete truthfulness that everything I have learned in my seventy-five years in this world, everything that has truly enhanced and enlightened my existence, has been through affliction and not through happiness, whether pursued or attained. In other words, if it ever were to be possible to eliminate affliction from our earthly existence by means of some drug or other medical mumbo jumbo, as Aldous Huxley envisaged in *Brave New World*, the result would not be to make life delectable, but to make it too banal and trivial to be endurable.[2]

If we go back to the theme of this chapter, we realize that there is more than one way to be prosperous: one according to God and the other according to man. The majority of people associate the word *prosperity* with economic boom, which is entirely wrong. Such is the case that not even the dictionary defines *prosperity* in that way. The *Oxford English Dictionary* defines prosperity as "the state of being prosperous," and *Merriam-Webster* defines it as "the condition of being successful or thriving."

These definitions say nothing about the financial part of life. However, when we speak of prosperity, everyone associates it with money. Now, what we can see in the second definition is that there is a connection between prosperity and the idea of having success. In fact, let us quote the second definition again, *"the condition of being successful or thriving."* Hence, for many, prosperity is synonymous with success. Therefore, for the purpose of developing the theme of this chapter, we will use the words *success* and *prosperity* interchangeably.

If prosperity is success in that which is undertaken, the question would then be: What is success? One of the dictionaries consulted defines success as obtaining "what is desired." If such is the case, we believe that there would be different definitions of what success is according to each person. Sadly, the way in which society defines success is very poorly focused due to the value system with which it lives. Steven Berglas, in his book *The Success Syndrome*, says that "Success, in America, is more than merely attaining what one wants; it is attaining a desired outcome that provides both a high level of material wealth and public recognition."[3]

Before going any further, let us remember that our society is highly materialistic, and this is important when it comes time to talk about the topic we are dealing with because a materialistic society is one that seeks to define a person as either a success or a failure. The man of today values that which is material over that which is spiritual, and this leads him to worry excessively over material things, which are those things that have no eternal value. Our society exhibits an attitude of discontent on all levels and at all ages: no one is content with his work, his wife, nor his salary, and even children complain about being bored. Boredom is a word that did not even exist generations ago. The *Oxford Old English Dictionary* mentions that the word *boredom* appears for the first time in 1852 in the novel *Bleak House* by Charles Dickens, although the attitude of being bored is noted prior to that time.[4] This causes our society to live with a continuous spirit of complaining and with an attitude of ingratitude. For this reason, men and women of today have placed an inordinate emphasis on material things, thinking that acquiring such things will calm their spirit of discontent. However, these conditions that we have just described are present both in prosperous individuals and in those who have not had success, something that allows us to clearly see that prosperity does not fulfill the true needs of man.

If we want to know the state or condition of our society, we only have to take note of how people define society or success, and then how they seek to live or display it.

Prosperity or Success According to Two Distinct Value Systems

For many, success or prosperity consists of the accumulation of material things, having a million dollars in the bank, or perhaps even more, having a nice house, a fine car, or a combination of all these things. For others, success consists of getting a master's degree or a doctorate in a particular area of study. For some, gaining success means having a high-level job at one of the best companies in the region. Independent of the aspirations of every person, the great majority considers that having success is like a combination of the five "P's" that we mentioned in chapter 7: prosperity, position, power, prestige, and pleasure.

This is how the human defines success and prosperity, which is not exactly how God defines it. They are two very different definitions of what success is and how to achieve it. In society, success is achieved by doing whatever is necessary in order to have prosperity, position, power, prestige, and pleasure. When society labels someone as successful, it usually evaluates these five characteristics and some others such as production, possessions, status, appearance, physical attractiveness, happiness, money, intelligence, etc. If we were to judge by these criteria, we would have to say that the person who has most influenced the world was a total failure. Of course, we are referring to the person of Christ, who during His life had neither prosperity nor position, neither power nor prestige; He did not seek pleasure nor did He have possessions, status, physical attractiveness, or worldly intelligence. However, there has never been a man as successful as He. Jesus is the person who has impacted the most lives. Because of His influence, history has been divided into "before Christ" and "after Christ." The impact of the person of Jesus on more than two thousand years of history has been monumental; nevertheless, to the eyes of the world, His life, which ended at thirty-three years of age, was a failure.

Every one of the qualities that the world recognizes as successful has to do with the outer world, but we must not forget what God revealed to the prophet Samuel in a moment in which he was focused on the external appearance of things. The Lord said to His prophet, "Do not look at his appearance or his stature because I have rejected him. Humans do not see what the LORD sees, for humans see what is visible, but the LORD sees the heart" (1 Sam. 16:7). Man lives concerned about the external and God about the internal. Humans live obsessed with having a good reputation, but God is interested in our first being concerned about our character. Remember, as we have already mentioned, that character represents what we are, our essence, that which is on the inside, while reputation is what others think we are. We must focus on cultivating our character, and God will then take care of our reputation.

Man's Motivation to Prosper

Before going any further, it might be worth it to ask ourselves: What is it that moves man to continually seek after success and prosperity? What moves him to seek after prestige, power, possession, position, popularity, and everything else? If we analyze well what the studies have revealed, we will realize that man is born with an immense need of approval; without such approval, he feels unhappy, insecure, incomplete, inferior, uneasy, and unsatisfied. Therefore, due to this inner dissatisfaction, he purposes to acquire things that will quench his thirst. He thinks that if he is financially prosperous, his prosperity will allow him to purchase material things that will earn the approval of those who measure success by appearances. Many think that if they buy a prestigious automobile, purchase a luxurious house, or acquire a certain position, they will be at the level of those with whom they can relate, this then causes them to seek after financial success.

For her part, the woman thinks that if she dresses in the latest fashion, she will attract men who are interested in her and that, when these men see how she looks, they will end up valuing and appreciating her for what she is. However, the opposite occurs. When a man is attracted simply by the way a woman looks, he learns to value her outer appearance and has no appreciation for who she really is. Hence, as the years pass by and the woman no longer looks like she did in her youth, the man starts looking in another direction.

There are people who realize their insecurity at some point and think that the way to feel safe is to buy insurance policies: life insurance, homeowner's insurance, medical insurance, and other similar products. But these policies cost money, and as they cost money, these people think that they have to be prosperous in order to buy security, which is impossible because nothing can protect them from an eventual natural disaster or sickness. Insurance policies provide money to repair damages caused by certain circumstances of life, but they do not prevent these circumstances.

Even the workaholism of our day is a reflection of the problems that we have been discussing. People work more to buy more or to feel like they are someone important in life. Those who feel inferior want to climb one rung higher on the ladder of success in order to feel like they are above someone else. In this way, we can make a whole list of the most common human motivations for success.

The human seeks the following:

- **Prosperity**, acquiring things that provide security. But as Solomon so well said, "The one who loves silver is never satisfied with silver, and whoever loves wealth is never satisfied with income. . . . When good things increase, the ones who consume them multiply" (Eccles. 5:10–11a).
- **A position of importance** in order not to feel inferior or under everyone else.
- **Power**, because this makes him feel that he is in control of everyone else.
- **Prestige** to fill the sense of void with which he is born.
- **Pleasure**, which he buys with money, seeking to anesthetize the pain with which he lives.
- **Possessions**, in order to impress others and be able to feel at their level. With said possessions, he seeks to communicate to others that he has been successful in life.
- **Improving his physical attractiveness**, because he wishes to feel that others seek after him, and if he succeeds, he intends to anesthetize his sense of loneliness.
- **Intelligence**, in order to demonstrate how much he knows and, therefore, how valuable he is. With his intelligence, man aims to acquire knowledge, and he frequently does so, but this will not fulfill him, either. What man needs is not knowledge; he needs wisdom. Knowledge allows us to live according to our purposes, but wisdom enables us to live according to God's purposes.
- **Feeling young** and, therefore, with a sense that he still can. Plastic surgery is no more than

an excessive effort by the man who is fighting
against the clock and does not want death to
come for him. The problem with plastic surgery
is that it makes the exterior look young but
leaves the interior intact.

- **Perpetuating a name.** This is why we see so
many philanthropists today who do works of
charity because they are seeking to perpetuate
a name so that they are not forgotten.

God created man with the sense of eternity in his heart, and
this sense should lead him to pursue his Creator. It is He who
transcends the "here and now." However, the man who has the
innate desire to be eternal instead of pursuing God, looks for
ways to extend his life—getting a suntan, taking vitamins, going
to the gym, researching how to slow the aging process—and as a
result, he has exchanged the image of the eternal God for temporary activities that continue to leave man without a sense of
purpose.

There is a story about a man who visited his psychiatrist
because he was depressed. After trying everything, the psychiatrist recommended that he go to a circus that had come to town,
where a clown worked who apparently made everyone laugh.
The psychiatrist said to him, "Every time I see this clown, he
has the unique ability to lift my spirit. Maybe he can help you
a bit with your depression." The patient said to the psychiatrist,
"Doctor, you do not understand; that clown is me!"[5] Obviously,
the clown was very successful, because the people came in mass
to see him and laugh, but he felt neither successful nor prosperous. What is seen is not always reality.

Rarely in society does anyone consider prosperity or success
in nonmaterial terms. Nevertheless, the question we must ask
ourselves is the following: If a man reaches a highly regarded
position and earns a lot of money but, in the process, he neglects
and loses his wife and children, can he consider himself a success? Some would say so, that he was successful in his career,

although he may have been a failure in his family. In fact, this is the reality for a large number of people in today's society. People who meet these conditions are considered successful only because our society is so materialistic.

On July 20, 1993, in Washington, D.C., Vincent Foster, who was the personal aide to President Bill Clinton, sat in the Rose Garden at the White House to listen to the president announce the resignation of the director of the FBI. Foster returned to his office after the ceremony, reviewed some legal documents, and after speaking to President Clinton, whom he had known since his youth, he had lunch at his desk. A little after one o'clock in the afternoon, he left his office and informed one of his aides that he would return. He left in his vehicle and drove to a small, federal park on the banks of the Potomac River. Once there, he got out of the vehicle carrying a revolver, stood near a cannon that pointed toward the forest, and, there, Vincent Foster took his life. When the president found out, he called his aides and said to them, "It would be wrong to define the life of Vincent Foster simply by how he died." And although this is true, it is no less true that it proves difficult to categorize a life as a success when it ends in suicide.

We cannot look exclusively at a person's job performance to define what prosperity or success is; we must look at the whole person. Therefore, I would like to propose a term that I came across recently. That term is *holistic integrity*, which can be defined as a person's ability to have success in all areas of life, including his character, family, and the world around him. One of the great problems of our generation is that it has not known how to prioritize its purposes, and, therefore, it has not known how to measure its level of success.

In March of 1991, the magazine *OMNI*, in the article "Why Successful People Fail," said that successful people suffered or were victims of the three "A's":

- Aloneness
- Adventure Seeking
- Adultery

The same magazine indicated that often, when a person appears to have it all, things suddenly seem to collapse, and everything becomes rubbish. Can we really classify as prosperity the condition of the human who is at the top of his career but feels alone, depressed, unsatisfied, and whose family is adrift at sea because of adultery? I do not believe so.

God defines prosperity and success in very different ways. When Moses died, Joshua succeeded him, and God wanted to define for him the way of success so that he would not deviate from it. This is what God said to him:

> Above all, be strong and very courageous to observe carefully the whole instruction my servant Moses commanded you. Do not turn from it to the right or the left, so that you will have success wherever you go. (Josh. 1:7)

For God, success and prosperity depend on obedience to His Word. Joshua had to learn the law and meditate on it day and night and obey it; only then would he prosper in his ways and have success. God defines prosperity distinctly from how the world defines it, and He expresses it in the following words of Jesus: "For what will it benefit someone if he gains the whole world yet loses his life? Or what will anyone give in exchange for his life?" (Matt. 16:26). In this world, prosperity usually means failure in the kingdom of heaven. If God created us with a purpose and at the end of our days we have not fulfilled that purpose, in God's eyes, we are an enormous failure. When someone says to us, "You are a failure," this is strong language; but when God tells us, "You are a failure because you did not fulfill my purposes," this is even stronger language.

In this book, we have established principles that are intimately related with what it means to be successful according to God's ways. In chapter 2, when we spoke about the necessity of having an organized inner world, what we taught there contributes to a successful life, spiritually speaking. We can say the same when we speak about cultivating a biblical mind (chapter 3) or of living a life of purpose (chapter 11) for the glory of God (chapter 8). Therefore, the rest of this chapter will be dedicated to discussing how not to become seduced by success.

Be a Servant Who Is Not Seduced by Success

The key to being a man of God who is not seduced by success is our identity in Christ. In the whole of history, there has never existed, nor will there ever exist, a man more successful than Jesus. The Word of God says that He was tempted in everything, but the world could not seduce Him. Jesus had a close relationship with His Father that not even temptations, nor power, nor privileges, nor misfortunes could take Him off course. He also did not need the famous "P's" that we discussed earlier to make Him feel that His life was really valuable. In my opinion, the following words allow us to see what a failure of a man is in the eyes of the world, but with the greatest success according to God's standards:

> Here is a man who was born in an obscure village, the child of a peasant woman. He grew up in another obscure village, where He worked in a carpenter shop until He was thirty, and then for three years He was an itinerant preacher. He never wrote a book. He never held an office. He never owned a home. He never had a family. He never went to college. He never put his foot inside a big city. He never traveled two hundred miles from the place where He was born. He never did one of the things that usually accompany greatness. He had no credentials but Himself. He had nothing to do with this world except the naked power of His divine manhood. While still a young man, the tide of public opinion turned

against Him. His friends ran away. One of them denied Him. He was turned over to His enemies. He went through the mockery of a trial. He was nailed to a cross between two thieves. His executioners gambled for the only piece of property He had on earth while He was dying—and that was His coat. When He was dead, He was taken down and laid in a borrowed grave through the pity of a friend. Nineteen wide centuries have come and gone [today, twenty centuries] and today He is the centerpiece of the human race and the leader of the column of progress. I am far within the mark when I say that all the armies that ever marched, and all the navies that ever were built, and all the parliaments that ever sat, all the kings that ever reigned, put together have not affected the life of man upon this earth as powerfully as has that One Solitary Life.[6]

Let us compare this story to that of nine men who, at their time, were considered the wealthiest men in the world. In 1923, these individuals met at the Edgewater Beach Hotel in the city of Chicago in the United States. It is estimated that their combined wealth exceeded that of the United States at the time. The following men attended this meeting:

1. The president of the largest steel company
2. The president of the largest utility company
3. The president of the largest gas company
4. The president of the New York Stock Exchange
5. The president of the Bank of International Settlements
6. The greatest wheat speculator
7. The greatest "bear" on Wall Street
8. The head of the world's greatest monopoly
9. A member of President Harding's cabinet

Nevertheless, it is sad to see what became of them twenty-five years later (1948):

1. The president of the then largest steel company (Bethlehem Steel Corp), Charles Schwab, lived on borrowed capital for five years before he died bankrupt.
2. The president of the largest utility company, Samuel Insull, died penniless.
3. The president of the then largest gas company, Howard Hudson, went insane.
4. Then president of the New York Stock Exchange, Richard Whitney, was sent to jail.
5. The president of the Bank of International Settlements, Leon Fraser, took his own life.
6. One of the greatest commodity traders (wheat speculator), Arthur Cutten, died insolvent.
7. The greatest "bear" on Wall Street, Jesse Livermore, committed suicide.
8. The president of the then world's greatest monopoly, Ivar Kreuger, also killed himself.
9. The member of US President Harding's cabinet, Albert Fall, was pardoned from jail just to be able to go home and die in peace.[7]

Jesus knew the past story of Solomon and the future stories of these nine men and many, many others. This is why He taught these words that the world still does not believe:

> Someone from the crowd said to him, "Teacher, tell my brother to divide the inheritance with me."
>
> "Friend," he said to him, "who appointed me a judge or arbitrator over you?" He then told them, "Watch out and be on guard against all

greed, because one's life is not in the abundance of his possessions."

Then he told them a parable: "A rich man's land was very productive. He thought to himself, 'What should I do, since I don't have anywhere to store my crops? I will do this,' he said. 'I'll tear down my barns and build bigger ones and store all my grain and my goods there. Then I'll say to myself, "You have many goods stored up for many years. Take it easy; eat, drink, and enjoy yourself."'

"But God said to him, 'You fool! This very night your life is demanded of you. And the things you have prepared—whose will they be?'

"That's how it is with the one who stores up treasure for himself and is not rich toward God." (Luke 12:13–21)

This parable of Jesus teaches us that greed is not a new sin; it is something that has been with man since the beginning. Humans spend more time and energy building a life in a temporary world than they do preparing for the life that is to come; they are rich in this life and poor in the coming kingdom.

Success according to God requires the following:

- Obtaining eternal life
- Living a life of obedience and dependence on God
- Fulfilling the purpose for which we were created
- Fighting the good fight and finishing the race
- Keeping the faith, just as the apostle Paul did

After writing to his disciple Timothy about how he had lived and finished the race well, Paul writes these words which truly describe success according to God, "There is reserved for me the crown of righteousness, which the Lord, the righteous Judge, will give me on that day, and not only to me, but to all those who have loved his appearing" (2 Tim. 4:8).

Earlier we mentioned that Jesus did not allow anyone or anything to deviate Him from God's plan because He had a very clear sense of His identity as the Son of God and the incarnate Messiah. In the same way, we must always remember this:

- Success does not define who we are. Our position in Christ does.
- What we do does not define who we are either, but what Christ did.
- Success may cost us dearly; sometimes it costs us everything.
- Most people violate their integrity on the ladder of success and, therefore, do not finish well.
- Success as a result is not a sin; the pursuit of it as our only objective is.

Solomon, even with all of his wisdom, did not know how to manage success. It was not that he simply did not know how to manage his wealth, but he also did know how to manage success. Solomon was (and will continue to be) the wisest man than fallen humanity has ever seen. Also, he was a businessman, an architect and builder, a millionaire; he was a man who possessed a fleet of ships, had a thousand women, became a famous writer and poet, was a musician and partook of every pleasure. Nevertheless, at the end of his days, he was still empty, and this led him to leave us the following recommendation:

> When all has been heard, the conclusion of the matter is this: fear God and keep his commands, because this is for all humanity. For God will bring every act to judgment, including every hidden thing, whether good or evil. (Eccles. 12:13–14)

At the beginning of this chapter, we shared a couple of definitions of success according to various dictionaries, but obviously, God inspired the Bible and not dictionaries. Therefore, God's definition of success is very different from those the secular dictionaries provide us. Kent and Barbara Hughes define success according to God in the following way:

- Success is faithfulness.
- Success is serving.
- Success is loving.
- Success is believing.
- Success is holiness.
- Success is attitude.

Each one of these statements represents a chapter from the book written by the Hughes couple titled *Liberating Ministry from the Success Syndrome.*[8] The chapter titles allow us to see how different God's opinion of success on earth is.

Final Reflection

At the end of this chapter on prosperity and success, I believe it is worth reflecting upon the words of Malcom Muggeridge in a speech he gave in 1985 titled "The True Crisis of Our Time." Muggeridge was a British journalist and intellectual who described himself as an agnostic for the majority of his life, but ultimately found Christ in 1969 and published his first book on Christ titled *Jesus Rediscovered.* These are the words of this great social analyst and intellectual:

> We look back on history, and what do we see? Empires rising and falling; revolutions and counter-revolutions succeeding one another; wealth accumulating and wealth dispersed; one nation dominant and then another. Shakespeare speaks

of "the rise and fall of great ones that ebb and flow with the moon."

In one lifetime I've seen my fellow country-men [Britons] ruling over a quarter of the world, and the great majority of them convinced—in the words of what is still a favorite song—that "God who's made the mighty will make them mightier yet."

I've heard a crazed, cracked Austrian [refer-ring to Hitler] proclaim to the world the estab-lishment of a German Reich that was to last for a thousand years; an Italian clown [referring to Mussolini] announce that he would restart the calendar to begin with his own assumption of power; a murderous Georgian brigand [referring to Stalin] in the Kremlin acclaimed by the intel-lectual elite of the Western world as wiser than Solomon, more enlightened than Ashoka [Indian emperor], more humane than Marcus Aurelius [Roman emperor].

I've seen America wealthier than all the rest of the world put together; and with the supe-riority of weaponry that would have enabled Americans, had they so wished, to outdo an Alexander or a Julius Caesar in the range and scale of conquest. All in one little lifetime—gone with the wind. England now part of an island off the coast of Europe, threatened with further dismemberment and bankruptcy. Hitler and Mussolini dead and remembered only in infamy. Stalin a sinister name in the regime he helped to found and dominated totally for three decades. Americans haunted by fears of running out of the precious fluid that keeps their motorways roaring and the smog settling, with troubled memories of a disastrous military campaign in Vietnam, and the great victory of the Don Quixotes of the media when they charged the windmills of Watergate . . .[9]

The speech continues and Muggeridge finishes by posing the following question: "Can this really be what life is about?"[10] More than thirty years have passed since Malcolm Muggeridge spoke these famous words. We now live in later times which are worse than those described by Muggeridge in a time which has been called the "post-Christian age"—a moment when the influence of Christian values plays no important role in the decisions of the majority of Western society.

It is precisely in moments like these when we cannot allow ourselves to be seduced by success nor by what the world would offer us nor by the schemes of the enemy. This will require a Christ-centered life, a biblical mind saturated by the Word, and a complete vertical focus in all of our life.

BIBLIOGRAPHY

Adams, Linda. "Learning a New Skill Is Easier Said Than Done." http://www.gordontraining.com/free-workplace-articles /learning-a-new-skill-is-easier-said-than-done/#.

Aristotle. *Politics (Part IV)*, translated by Benjamin Jowett. http://classics.mit.edu/Aristotle/politics.3.three.html.

Barclay, William. *The New Daily Study Bible: The Letters to the Philippians, Colossians, and Thessalonians*, revised edition. Louisville: Westminster, 1975.

Bartholomew, Craig G. *Ecclesiastes (Baker Commentary on the Old Testament Wisdom and Psalms)* Tremper Longman III, ed. Grand Rapids: Baker Academic, 2009.

Berglas, Steven. *The Success Syndrome: Hitting Bottom When You Reach the Top*, 1st edition. New York: Springer, 1986.

Blackaby, Henry T. and Roy T. Edgemon. *The Ways of God: How God Reveals Himself Before a Watching World.* Nashville: B&H Publishers, 2000.

Blamires, Harry. *The Christian Mind.* Vancouver, BC: Regent College Publishing, 2005.

Blowe, Vendetta. *R.I.P.: Rebellion, Idolatry, Pride = A Spiritual Death Sentence.* Enumclaw, WA: Pleasant Word, a division of WinePress Publishing Group, 2007.

Boice, James Montgomery. *Romans,* Vol. 4. Grand Rapids: Baker Books, 1995.

Bruce, A. B. *The Training of the Twelve.* Grand Rapids: Kregel Publications, 1971.

Butler, John G. *Moses: The Emancipator.* Clinton, IA: LBC Publications, 1996.

Calvin, John. *Institutes of the Christian Religion.*

Carlyle, Thomas. *On Heroes, Hero-Worship, and the Heroic in History: Six Lectures.* New York: Wiley and Putnam, 1846.

Carroll, Lewis. *Alice's Adventures in Wonderland.* 18th Century Editors, 2012.

Chester, Tim. *You Can Change.* Wheaton: Crossway, 2010.

Ciampa, Roy E. *The First Letter to the Corinthians,* The Pillar New Testament Commentary. Grand Rapids: Wm. B. Eerdmans, 2010.

Clinton, Robert. *The Making of a Leader.* Colorado Springs: NavPress, 1988.

Colson, Charles. *The Problem of Ethics.* Speech given at Harvard Business School in April of 1991.

Diccionario expositivo de palabras del Antiguo y del Nuevo Testamento de Vine. Nashville: Grupo Nelson, 2007.

Eisenhower, Dwight D. "The Best Dwight D. Eisenhower Quotes." Accessed January 11, 2017. https://www.brainyquote .com/quotes/quotes/d/dwightdei124736.html.

Engstrom, Ted W. *The Making of a Christian Leader.* Grand Rapids: Zondervan, 1978.

Farrar, Steve. *Finishing Strong.* Sisters, OR: Multnomah Publishers, Inc., 1995.

Fee, Gordon. *The First Epistle to the Corinthians,* The New International Commentary on the New Testament. Grand Rapids: Wm. B. Eerdmans, 2014.

Foster, Richard. *The Celebration of Discipline,* 3rd edition. San Francisco: HarperSanFrancisco, 1998.

Francis, James Allan. *One Solitary Life,* pp. 1–7 (1963). Accessed January 10, 2017. http://www.bartleby.com/73/916.html.

Garden, Allen. *Puritan Christianity in America.* Grand Rapids: Baker, 1990.

Garland, David E. *Philippians,* The Expositor Bible Commentary, revised edition, Vol. 12. Grand Rapids: Zondervan, 2006.

Gellman, Marc. "How We See Sharon—and Israel." *Newsweek,* January 9, 2005. Accessed January 14, 2017. http://europe.newsweek.com/how-we-see-sharon-and-israel-108309?rm=eu.

Harmon, Matthew. *Philippians: A Mentor Commentary.* Great Britain: Christian Focus Publications, 2015.

Hughes, Kent and Barbara. *Liberating Ministry from the Success Syndrome.* Wheaton: Crossway, 2008.

Hughes, Kent. *Disciplines of a Godly Man.* Wheaton: Crossway Books, 2001.

———. *Philippians.* Wheaton: Crossway Books, 2007.

Inrig, Gary. *A Call to Excellence.* Wheaton: Victor Books, 1985.

Jones, Robert D. *Uprooting Anger.* Phillipsburg, NJ: P&R Publishing, 2005.

Keller, Timothy. *Every Good Endeavor.* New York: Penguin Group, Inc., 2012.

Kittel, Gerhard and Gerhard Friedrich. *Theological Dictionary of the New Testament,* in *doxa.* Grand Rapids: Wm. B. Eerdmans Publishing Company, 1985.

Lanem, Timothy S. and Paul David Tripp. *How People Change.* Greensboro, NC: New Growth Press, 2008.

Lloyd-Jones, Martyn. *Studies in the Sermon on the Mount.* Grand Rapids: Wm. B. Eerdmans Publishing Company, 1976.

Luther, Martin. *Luther Lecture* on Romans. Edited by Wilhelm Pauck. Louisville: Westminster John Knox Press, 1961.

MacArthur, John. *Slave: The Hidden Truth about Your Identity in Christ.* Nashville: Thomas Nelson, 2012.

Maxwell, John. *The 21 Indispensable Qualities of a Leader,* 2nd edition. Nashville: Thomas Nelson, 2007.

McGrath, Alister E. *Reformation Thought: An Introduction,* 4th edition. West Sussex, UK: John Wiley & Sons, 2012.

Miller, Darrow L. *LifeWork: A Biblical Theology for What You Do Every Day.* Seattle: YWAM Publishing, 2009.

Mohler, Albert. "The Scandal of Biblical Illiteracy: It's Our Problem." Christian Headlines.com. Accessed January 2, 2017. http://www.christianheadlines.com/columnists/al -mohler/the-scandal-of-biblical-illiteracy-its-our9-problem -1270946.html.

———. "The Way the World Thinks: Meeting the Natural Mind in the Mirror and in the Marketplace" in *Thinking, Loving,*

Doing. Edited by John Piper and David Mathis. Wheaton: Crossway, 2011.

Moreland, J. P. *Love Your God with All Your Mind.* Colorado: NavPress, 1997.

Morley, Patrick. *The Man in the Mirror: Solving the 24 Problems Men Face.* Grand Rapids: Zondervan, 2002.

Muggeridge, Malcolm. *A 20th Century Testimony.* Nashville: Thomas Nelson, 1978.

————. "But Not of Christ." *Seeing Through the Eye: Malcolm Muggeridge on Faith.* Edited by Cecil Kuhne. San Francisco: Ignatius Press, 2005.

Murray, Andrew. *Humility: The Beauty of Holiness.* Abbotsford: Aneko Press, 2016.

Naugle, David K. *Worldview: The History of a Concept.* Grand Rapids: Wm. B. Eerdmans Publishing Company, 2002.

Noll, Mark. *The Scandal of the Evangelical Mind.* Grand Rapids: Wm. B. Eerdmans 1995.

Northouse, Peter G. *Leadership: Theory and Practice*, 7th edition. Thousand Oaks: SAGE Publications, Inc., 2015.

O'Donnell, Douglas Sean. *Ecclesiastes: Reformed Expository Commentary.* Phillipsburg, NJ: P&R Publishing, 2014.

Ojo, Fola. "Money by All Means Necessary? What a Miserable Life after All!" Accessed January 12, 2017. https://www.nairaland .com/2305129/1923-wealthiest-people-world-what.

Paliwoda, Daniel. *Melville and the Theme of Boredom.* Jefferson, NC: McFarland & Company, Inc., Company, 2010.

Pentecost, J. Dwight. *The Joy of Living: A Study of First John.* Grand Rapids: Lamplighter Books, 1973.

Piper, John. "Books Don't Change People, Paragraphs Do." Desiring God, July 16, 2013. Accessed January 9, 2017. http://www.desiringgod.org/articles/books-don-t-change -people-paragraphs-do.

————. *John G. Paton: You Will Be Eaten By Cannibals!* Minneapolis: Desiring God, 2012. http://www.desiringgod.org/books/ john-g-paton.

————. "The War against the Soul and the Glory of God." Preached May 22, 1994. Transcript and audio available at: http://www.desiringgod.org/messages/the-war-against -the-soul-and-the-glory-of-god.

Ramachandra, Vinoth. *Gods That Fail.* Westmont, IL: InterVarsity Press, 1996.

Ryken, Phillip Graham. *Exodus.* Wheaton: Crossway Books, 2005.

Ryken, Phillip Graham. *Galatians, Reformed Expository Commentary.* Phillipsburg, NJ: P & R Publishing, 2005.

Sanders, Oswald. *Spiritual Leadership.* Chicago: Moody Press, 1994.

Scazzeno, Peter. *The Emotionally Healthy Leader.* Grand Rapids: Zondervan, 2015.

Schopenhauer, Arthur. *The World as Will and Representation.* New York: Dover Publications, Inc., 1958.

Seifrid, Mark A. *The Second Letter to the Corinthians.* Grand Rapids: Wm. B. Eerdmans Publishing Company, 2014.

Spurgeon, Charles. *John Ploughman's Talk: Or Plain Advice for Plain People.* Chicago: Bible Institute Colportage Association, 1898.

―――. "The Heart of the Gospel." Sermon preached on the Lord's Day Morning, July 28, 1886, at Metropolitan Tabernacle of Newington, London. https://www.spurgeon .org/resource-library/sermons/the-heart-of-the-gospel/.

Stott, John. *La fe cristiana frente a los desafíos contemporáneos* [The Christian Faith in the Face of Contemporary Challenges] Colorado Springs: InterVarsity Press, 1995.

Swindoll, Charles. *Diario de un viajero desesperado.* Miami: Editorial Betania, 1989.

―――. *The Tale of the Tardy Oxcart.* Nashville: Thomas Nelson, 1998.

Thielman, Frank. *Ephesians.* Grand Rapids: Baker Academics, 2010.

Tozer, A. W. "The Great God Entertainment." *The Best of A. W. Tozer.* Baker Book House, 1978.

―――. *The Root of the Righteous.* Chicago: Moody Publishers, 2015.

―――. "The Saint Must Walk Alone." *The Best of A. W. Tozer.* Baker Book House, 1978.

Verbrugge, Verlyn D. *The Expositor Bible Commentary* (1 Corinthians), Tremper Longman III & David E. Garland. Grand Rapids: Zondervan, 2008.

Washer, Paul. *The Gospel's Power and Message.* Grand Rapids: Reformation Heritage Books, 2012.

Welch, Edward T. *When People Are Big and God Is Small: Overcoming Peer Pressure, Codependency, and the Fear of Man.* Phillipsburg, NJ: P&R Publishing, 1997.

Wiersbe, Warren. *Ephesians through Revelation*, The Bible Exposition Commentary, Vol. 2. Colorado Springs: Victor, Cook Communications Ministries.

———. *On Being a Servant of God.* Grand Rapids: Baker Books, 2007.

———. *Ten Power Principles for Christian Service.* Grand Rapids: Baker Books, 2008.

Willard, Dallas. *Renovation of the Heart: Putting on the Character of Christ.* Colorado Springs: NavPress, 2002.

Williams, Ray. "The Decline of Fatherhood and the Male Identity Crisis." *Psychology Today,* June 19, 2011.

NOTES

Chapter I: You Must Be before You Do

1. Verlyn D. Verbrugge, Tremper Longman III, and David E. Garland, *The Expositor Bible Commentary* (1 Corinthians) (Grand Rapids: Zondervan, 2008), 282.

2. Andrew Murray, *Humility: The Beauty of Holiness* (Abbotsford, WI: Aneko Press, 2016), 75.

3. Rabbi Schmuel ben Nachmani, *Talmudic tractate Berakhot* (55b), quoted in Marc Gellman, "How We See Sharon–and Israel," *Newsweek,* January 9, 2005, accessed on January 14, 2017, http://europe.newsweek.com/how-we-see-sharon-and-israel-108309?rm=eu.

4. Peter Scazzero, *The Emotionally Healthy Leader* (Grand Rapids: Zondervan, 2015), 56.

5. Chester, *You Can Change,* 83.

6. Robert D. Jones, *Uprooting Anger (*Phillipsburg, NJ: P&R Publishing, 2005), 17.

7. Tim Chester, *You Can Change* (Wheaton, IL: Crossway, 2010), 28.

8. See Edward T. Welch, *When People Are Big and God Is Small: Overcoming Peer Pressure, Codependency, and the Fear of Man* (Phillipsburg, NJ: P&R Publishing, 1997).

9. Attributed to Aristotle in *Politics,* translated by Benjamin Jowett (Part IV), http://classics.mit.edu/Aristotle/politics.3.three.html.

10. Developed by Noel Burch of Gordon Training International (GTI) over a period of thirty years. See Linda Adams, president of GTI, "Learning a New Skill is Easier Said Than Done," http://www.gordontraining.com/free-workplace-articles/learning-a-new-skill-is-easier-said-than-done/.

11. Timothy S. Lane and Paul David Tripp, *How People Change* (Greensboro, NC: New Growth Press, 2008), 63–78.

Chapter 2: Be a Servant Whose Inner World Is in Order

1. David K. Naugle, *Worldview: The History of a Concept* (Grand Rapids: Wm. B. Eerdmans Publishing Company, 2002), 64–66.

2. Frank Thielman, *Ephesians* (Grand Rapids: Baker Academics, 2010), 357.

3. From the sermon by Dr. John Piper, "The War Against the Soul and the Glory of God," preached May 22, 1994. Transcript and audio available at: http://www.desiringgod.org/messages/the-war-against-the-soul-and-the-glory-of-god.

4. Patrick Morley, *The Man in the Mirror* (Grand Rapids: Zondervan, 2014), 207–8.

Chapter 3: Be a Biblically Minded Servant

1. Quoted by Dr. Albert Mohler, "The Scandal of Biblical Illiteracy: It's Our Problem," Christian Headlines.com, accessed January 2, 2017, http://www.christianheadlines.com/columnists/al-mohler/the-scandal-of-biblical-illiteracy-its-our-problem-1270946.html.

2. Mark Noll, *The Scandal of the Evangelical Mind* (Grand Rapids: Wm. B. Eerdmans, 1995).

3. John Calvin, *Institutes of the Christian Religion*, 1.2.2.

4. Adapted from *La fe cristiana frente a los desafíos contemporáneos* [*The Christian Faith in the Face of Contemporary Challenges*] (Colorado Springs: InterVarsity Press, 1995).

5. Martin Luther, *Luther Lectures on Romans*, ed. by Wilhelm Pauck (Louisville, KY: Westminster John Knox Press, 1961), 159.

6. John Calvin, *Institutes of the Christian Religion*, 1.17.6.

7. Albert Mohler, "The Way the World Thinks: Meeting the Natural Mind in the Mirror and in the Marketplace" in *Thinking. Loving. Doing.*, ed. by John Piper and David Mathis (Wheaton: Crossway, 2011), 56.

8. Harry Blamires, "The Concept of a Christian Mind," *The Christian Mind* (Vancouver, BC: Regent College Publishing, 2005), 67–188.

9. Allen Garden, *Puritan Christianity in America* (Grand Rapids: Baker, 1990).

10. J. P. Moreland, *Love Your God with All Your Mind* (Colorado Springs: NavPress, 1997), 22–32.

11. Ibid., 29.

12. Ibid., 28.

Chapter 4: Be a Set-Apart Servant

1. See *ekklesia* (from *ek*, "out of," and *klesis*, "call" from *kaleo*, "to call") in *Diccionario expositivo de palabras del Antiguo y Nuevo Testamento de Vine* [Vine's *Expository Dictionary of Old and New Testament Words*] (Nashville: Thomas Nelson, 2007), 25.

2. A. W. Tozer, "The Saint Must Walk Alone," in *The Best of A. W. Tozer* (Grand Rapids: Baker Book House, 1978), 198.

3. Charles Spurgeon, *John Ploughman's Talk: Or Plain Advice for Plain People* (Chicago: Bible Institute Colportage Association, 1898), 47.

4. A. W. Tozer, "The Great God Entertainment," in *The Best of A. W. Tozer* (Grand Rapids: Baker Book House, 1978), 127.

5. Warren Wiersbe, *Ten Powerful Principles for Christian Service* (Grand Rapids: Baker Books, 2008), 39.

Chapter 5: Be a Servant of His Presence

1. Phillip Graham Ryken, *Exodus* (Wheaton: Crossway Books, 2005), 974.

2. Henry T. Blackaby and Roy T. Edgemon, *The Ways of God: How God Reveals Himself Before a Watching World* (Nashville: B&H Publishers, 2000), 83.

3. John G. Butler, *Moses: The Emancipator* (Clinton, IA: LBC Publications, 1996), 569.

4. Quoted by Charles Swindoll on the topic "God's Mercy," in *The Tale of The Tardy Oxcart* (Nashville: Thomas Nelson, 1998).

5. James Montgomery Boice, *Romans*, Vol. 4 (Grand Rapids: Baker Books, 1995), 1559.

Chapter 6: Be a Servant of a Life Well-Lived

1. Gordon Fee, *The First Epistle to the Corinthians*, The New International Commentary on the New Testament (Grand Rapids: Wm. B. Eerdmans, 2014), 538.

2. Roy E. Ciampa, *The First Letter to the Corinthians*, The Pillar New Testament Commentary (Grand Rapids: Wm. B. Eerdmans, 2010), 438–39.

3. Henry Blackaby, *Spiritual Leadership* (Nashville: Broadman & Holman Publishers, 2001), 126–27.

4. Gerhard Kittel and Gerhard Friedrich, *Theological Dictionary of the New Testament*, on *doxa* (Grand Rapids: Wm. B. Eerdmans Publishing Company, 1985), 178.

5. Herman Melville, quoted by Steve Farrar in *Finishing Strong* (Sisters, OR: Multnomah Publishers, Inc., 1995), 167.

6. Steve Farrar, *Finishing Strong: Going the Distance for Your Family* (Sisters, OR: Multnomah Publishers, Inc., 1995), 13–53.

7. Ibid., 13–15.

Chapter 7: Be a Servant Shaped by the Gospel

1. Paul Washer, *The Gospel's Power and Message* (Grand Rapids: Reformation Heritage Books, 2012), viii.

2. Charles Spurgeon, "The Heart of the Gospel" (sermon preached the morning of the Lord's Day, July 28, 1886, at the Metropolitan Tabernacle, Newington, London), https://www.spurgeon.org/resource -library/sermons/the-heart-of-the-gospel/.

3. Dallas Willard, *Renovation of the Heart: Putting on the Character of Christ* (Colorado Springs: NavPress, 2002), 238.

4. Phillip Graham Ryken, *Galatians, Reformed Expository Commentary* (Phillipsburg: P&R Publishing, 2005), 232.

5. Mark A. Seifrid, *The Second Letter to the Corinthians* (Grand Rapids: Wm. B. Eerdmans Publishing Company, 2014), 247.

Chapter 8: Be a Servant for His Glory

1. David E. Garland, *Philippians, The Expositor's Bible Commentary*, revised edition, Vol. 12 (Grand Rapids: Zondervan, 2006), 216.

2. John MacArthur, *Slave: The Hidden Truth about Your Identity in Christ* (Nashville: Thomas Nelson, 2012), 15.

3. A job counselor, quoted by Warren Wiersbe in *Ephesians through Revelation*, The Bible Exposition Commentary, Vol. 2, (Colorado Springs: Victor, Cook Communications Ministries), 74.

4. Kent Hughes, *Philippians* (Wheaton: Crossway Books, 2007), 82–83.

5. Warren W. Wiersbe, *On Being a Servant of God* (Grand Rapids: Baker Books, 2007), 12.

6. Quoted by Warren Wiersbe in *On Being a Servant of God* (Grand Rapids: Baker Books, 2007), 46.

Chapter 9: Be a Spiritual Servant

1. Ray Williams, "The Decline of Fatherhood and the Male Identity Crisis" in *Psychology Today*, June 19, 2011. Note: the author was citing statistics from *Fatherless America* by David Blankenhorn.

2. John Maxwell, *The 21 Indispensable Qualities of a Leader*, 2nd edition (Nashville: Thomas Nelson, 2007), xi.

3. Ibid., 5.

4. Peter G. Northouse, *Leadership: Theory and Practice,* 7th edition (Thousand Oaks, CA: SAGE Publications, Inc., 2015), 6.

5. Oswald Sanders, *Spiritual Leadership* (Chicago: Moody Press, 1994), 27.

6. Robert Clinton, *The Making of a Leader* (Colorado Springs: NavPress 1988), 26.

7. Henry Blackaby, *Spiritual Leadership* (Nashville: Broadman & Holman Publishers, 2001), 20.

8. A. B. Bruce, *The Training of the Twelve* (Grand Rapids: Kregel Publications, 1971), 296.

9. Warren Wiersbe, *Ten Power Principles for Christian Service* (Grand Rapids: Baker Books, 2008).

Chapter 10: Be a Servant of Influence

1. Charles Colson, "The Problem of Ethics" (speech given at Harvard Business School, April 1991).

2. Vendetta Blowe, *R.I.P.: Rebellion, Idolatry, Pride = A Spiritual Death Sentence* (Enumclaw, WA: Pleasant Word, a division of WinePress Publishing Group, 2007).

3. J. Dwight Pentecost, *The Joy of Living: A Study of First John* (Grand Rapids: Lamplighter Books, 1973), 55.

4. William Barclay, *The New Daily Study Bible: The Letters to the Philippians, Colossians, and Thessalonians*, revised edition (Louisville: Westminster, 1975), 37.

5. D. Martyn Lloyd-Jones, *Studies in the Sermon on the Mount* (Grand Rapids: Wm. B. Eerdmans Publishing Company, 1976), 58.

Chapter 11: Be a Servant of Purpose

1. Arthur Schopenhauer, *The World as Will and Representation* (New York: Dover Publications, Inc., 1958), 196.

2. Malcolm Muggeridge, *Jesus Rediscovered*, quoted by Douglas Sean O'Donnell in *Ecclesiastes: Reformed Expository Commentary* (Phillipsburg, NJ: P&R Publishing, 2014), 42–43.

3. Douglas Sean O'Donnell, *Ecclesiastes: Reformed Expository Commentary* (Phillipsburg: P&R Publishing, 2014), 48–49.

4. Ibid.

5. John Ruskin, English artist and art critic.

6. Craig G. Bartholomew, *Ecclesiastes (Baker Commentary on the Old Testament Wisdom and Psalms)*, Tremper Longman III, ed., Kindle Edition, Loc. 2442 of 14425 (Grand Rapids: Baker Academic, 2009).

7. Patrick Morley, *The Man in the Mirror* (Grand Rapids: Zondervan, 2014), Kindle Edition, 34–35, Location 399 of 5880.

8. Jim Elliot (1927–1956) was an evangelical missionary who was martyred along with four other persons while trying to reach the Auca tribe in Ecuador with the gospel.

9. John Piper, *John G. Paton: You Will Be Eaten by Cannibals!* (Minneapolis: Desiring God, 2012), 6, http://desiringgod.org/books/john-g-paton.

Chapter 12: Be a Servant Who Lives His Call

1. Alister E. McGrath, *Reformation Thought: An Introduction*, 4th Edition (West Sussex, UK: John Wiley & Sons, 2012), 257.

2. Timothy Keller, *Every Good Endeavor* (New York: Penguin Group, Inc., 2012), 39.

3. Ibid., 41.

4. Darrow L. Miller, *LifeWork: A Biblical Theology for What You Do Every Day* (Seattle: YWAM Publishing, 2009), 104.

5. Lewis Carroll, *Alice's Adventures in Wonderland* (19th Century Editors, 2012), 69.

6. See chapter 2 on how to be a servant whose inner world is in order.

7. Matthew Harmon, *Philippians: A Mentor Commentary* (Great Britain: Christian Focus Publications, 2015), 177.

Chapter 13: Be a Reflexive Servant

1. Richard Foster, *The Celebration of Discipline*, 3rd edition (San Francisco: HarperSanFrancisco, 1998), 1.

2. John Piper, "Books Don't Change People, Paragraphs Do," *Desiring God*, July 16, 2013, accessed January 9, 2017, http://www.desiringgod.org/articles/books-don't-change-people-paragraphs-do.

3. Ted W. Engstrom, *The Making of a Christian Leader* (Grand Rapids: Zondervan, 1978), 199.

4. Dwight D. Eisenhower, "The Best Dwight D. Eisenhower Quotes," accessed January 11, 2017, https://brainyquote.com/quotes/quotes/d/dwightdei124736.html.

5. Quote attributed to D. L. Moody.

6. Gary Inrig, *A Call to Excellence* (Wheaton: Victory Books, 1985), 98.

7. Vinoth Ramachandra, *Gods that Fail* (Westmont, IL: InterVarsity Press, 1996), 174.

8. A. W. Tozer, *The Root of the Righteous* (Chicago: Moody Publishers, 2015), 165.

Chapter 14: Be a Servant Who Is Not Seduced by Success

1. Thomas Carlyle, *On Heroes, Hero-Worship, and the Heroic in History: Six Lectures* (New York: Wiley and Putnam, 1846), 174. Available at HathiTrust: https://hdl.handle.net/2027/nyp.33433074966502.

2. Malcolm Muggeridge, *A Twentieth Century Testimony* (Nashville: Thomas Nelson, 1978), 35.

3. Steven Berglas, *The Success Syndrome: Hitting Bottom When You Reach the Top*, 1st edition (New York: Springer, 1986), 6.

4. Daniel Paliwoda, *Melville and the Theme of Boredom* (Jefferson, NC: McFarland & Company, Inc., 2010), 15.

5. Adaptation of the story narrated by Charles Swindoll in his book *Living on the Ragged Edge* translated to Spanish as *Diario de un viajero desesperado* (Miami: Editorial Betania, 1989), 42.

6. James Allan Francis, *One Solitary Life*, pages 1–7 (1963), accessed January 10, 2017, http://www.bartleby.com/73/916.html.

7. Fola Ojo, "Money by All Means Necessary? What a Miserable Life After All!" accessed January 12, 2017, https://www.nairaland.com/2305129/1923-wealthiest-people-world-what.

8. Kent and Barbara Hughes, *Liberating Ministry from the Success Syndrome* (Wheaton: Crossway, 2008).

9. Malcolm Muggeridge, "But Not of Christ," in *Seeing Through the Eye: Malcolm Muggeridge on Faith*, ed. Cecil Kuhne (San Francisco: Ignatius Press, 2005), 29–30.

10. Ibid.